Ken Hom's
QUICK AND EASY
Chinese
COOKERY

For Gerry Cavanaugh, Gordon Wing
and Mimi Luebbermann

Born in the United States, Ken Hom first learnt the fundamental Chinese cookery techniques in his uncle's restaurant in Chicago. Now an internationally acclaimed teacher, chef, consultant and writer on food and travel, he regulary conducts cookery classes throughout the world.

Ken Hom is also the author of *Ken Hom's Vegetable and Pasta Book, East Meets West* and *A Taste of China*. He has been described by the food editor of the *New York Times* as 'one of the world's leading authorities on Chinese cooking'. He divides his time between Europe, California and Hong Kong.

Ken Hom's
QUICK AND EASY
Chinese
COOKERY

BBC BOOKS

A QUICK & EASY ACKNOWLEDGEMENT

I am grateful to Gerry Cavanaugh, who so ably assists me in organising my thoughts into a coherent message; Gordon Wing, who works side by side with me to make a recipe as perfect as possible; and finally Mimi Luebbermann, whose exacting editing of the recipes and experience contribute to a better book.

I owe thanks to the expert staff of BBC Books, and in particular to Nick Chapman and Nina Shandloff – who both commissioned this book – and also to Heather Holden-Brown and Susan Martineau for their much appreciated editing skills.

And as always to Ted Lyman and Martha Casselman.

PHOTOGRAPHY *Monique Le Luhandre*
FOOD PREPARATION *Berit Vinegrad*
STYLING *Rebecca Gillies*
ILLUSTRATIONS *Teresa O'Brien*

Published by BBC Books
A division of BBC Enterprises Ltd
Woodlands, 80 Wood Lane
London W12 0TT

First published 1989
Reprinted 1991 (twice)
Reprinted 1992

ISBN 0 563 20675 6

Typeset in 10½/13pt Cheltenham Light and printed
and bound in England by Mackays of Chatham PLC
Colour origination by Technik Ltd, Berkhamsted
Colour printed by Lawrence Allen
Cover printed by Clays Ltd, St Ives plc

CONTENTS

All these are approximate conversions, which have been rounded either up or down. In a few recipes it has been necessary to modify them very slightly. Never mix metric and imperial measures in one recipe. Stick to one system or the other.

Weights

½ oz	10 g
1	25
1½	40
2	50
3	75
4	110
5	150
6	175
7	200
8	225
9	250
10	275
12	350
13	375
14	400
15	425
1 lb	450
1¼	550
1½	700
2	900
3	1.4 kg
4	1.8
5	2.3

Volume

1 fl oz	25 ml
2	50
3	75
5 (¼ pint)	150
10 (½)	300
15 (¾)	400
1 pint	570
1¼	700
1½	900
1¾	1 litre
2	1.1
2¼	1.3
2½	1.4
2¾	1.6
3	1.7
3¼	1.8
3½	2
3¾	2.1
4	2.3
5	2.8
6	3.4
7	4.0
8 (1 gal)	4.5

Measurements

¼ inch	0.5 cm
½	1
1	2.5
2	5
3	7.5
4	10
6	15
7	18
8	20.5
9	23
11	28
12	30.5

Oven temperatures

Mk	°F	°C
1	275°F	140°C
2	300	150
3	325	170
4	350	180
5	375	190
6	400	200
7	425	220
8	450	230
9	475	240

INTRODUCTION

*A*ll the recipes and menus in this book are designed for simplicity and rapidity of preparation. We need to be clear that 'quick and easy' entails no sacrifice of quality. It does not imply machine-made 'fast food'. It means only that the more elaborate and time-consuming recipes and menus of Chinese cookery have been omitted or re-fashioned in order to expedite the preparation of authentic and delectable meals. The essence remains the same; only the element of time has been changed.

Cooking quickly and easily comes naturally to those who spend a good deal of time in the kitchen. Of course, it is to be expected that elaborate multi-course dinners take much more time and effort. But not every meal is a major social or family event, no cook *always* has enough time, and sometimes, perhaps more often than not, a quick, easy, delectable, authentic meal is just the right thing. The preparation of such meals is what this book is about.

I have been developing these quick and easy recipes and techniques over the years, and more so of late, as my professional responsibilities have encroached upon my available kitchen time. Freshness of central ingredients remains my primary concern. I have, however, employed alternative techniques and allowed for substitution of secondary ingredients.

This has not been as difficult as it might seem. Except for a few sauces and seasonings, authentic Chinese cookery does not depend so much upon ingredients in the way, for example, that Japanese cookery does. Thus tomatoes, corn, potatoes, sweet potatoes, asparagus and a host of 'alien' foods have been readily accepted into Chinese cookery. Remember, too, that not all processed foods are to be scorned: tinned tomatoes are an excellent substitute for fresh ones, and frozen vegetables are sometimes superior to (and cheaper than) fresh but out-of-season varieties. Thus we may substitute Western or processed ingredients if necessary or desirable.

Refinements of techniques matter very much, but they too may be modified or adjusted as the food or time available permit. Pressure-cookers, electric mixers, slow-cookers, food processors and even microwave ovens have been accepted into 'authentic' Chinese kitchens. These are all time and energy savers, all perfectly acceptable to use – after all, even the wok was once an innovation.

There are very basic reasons why Chinese cookery is popular the world over: technique and a few essential seasonings can make everyone's native foods into 'Chinese'. These same virtues make for excellent 'quick and easy' food. What matters, once your pantry is stocked, is organisation, the right recipes and experience. Use this book as a point of departure. When you shop, do it when you can take your time: savour the experience of building your pantry. Note that some of the recipes have a longer list of ingredients than you might expect in a 'quick and easy' cookbook: this is essential to capture the flavours of authentic good cooking. Even 'quick and easy' food requires your attention – but there are few things in this world more worthy of your time and concern or more rewarding.

BASIC CHINESE PANTRY

Quick and easy cookery is, well, quick and easy once you have at hand the basics of a Chinese pantry. These items, no longer exotic, are readily available in supermarkets and speciality food shops. And there need be very little waste involved in stocking up your store-cupboard as almost every one of these basic ingredients will keep nicely for a long time. You will have to shop only for fresh ingredients – those given in the Shopping List at the beginning of each recipe; it is assumed that, having read this section, you will already have the staples, so these are not drawn to your attention in the same way.

Remember too that if your pantry lacks an ingredient, something else can almost certainly substitute for it. Perhaps soy sauce is the only seasoning whose flavour cannot be replaced. Everything else resolves itself to a matter of taste, *your* taste. You are in command!

BEAN CURD

Bean curd is also known by its Chinese name, *dou foo* (*dofu*), or by its Japanese name, *tofu*. It has played an important part in Chinese cookery for over 1000 years because it is highly nutritious, rich in protein, and goes well with other foods. Bean curd has a distinctive texture but a bland taste. It is made from yellow soya beans which are soaked, ground, mixed with water and then cooked briefly before being solidified. It is usually sold in two forms: in a firm cake or in a soft custard-like form. It is perfect for quick and easy meals because it is so versatile, needs little cooking, and can easily be combined with other foods. It is also quite inexpensive. The soft bean curd (sometimes called silken *tofu*) is used for soups and other dishes, while the firm type is used for stir-frying, braising and deep-frying. Firm bean curd 'cakes', white in colour, are sold in many supermarkets, health food shops and Asian grocers'. They are packed in water in plastic containers and may be kept in this state in the refrigerator for up to 5 days, provided the water is changed daily. To use firm bean curd, cut the required amount into cubes or shreds using a sharp knife. Do this with care as it is delicate. It also needs to be cooked gently as too much stirring can cause it to disintegrate. This does not, however, affect its nutritional value.

BLACK BEANS

These small black soya beans, also known as salted black beans or fermented black beans, are preserved by being fermented with salt and spices. They have a distinctive, slightly salty taste and a pleasantly rich smell and are used as a seasoning, often in conjunction with garlic or fresh root ginger. This appetite-stimulating aroma can quickly transform an ordinary fast meal into something special. Black beans can be combined with a number of foods to give them a deep rich flavour. They are inexpensive and increasingly easier to obtain; I see them often in supermarkets. Although you can buy them in tins as 'black beans in salted sauce', you may also see them packed in plastic bags, and these are preferable. The beans are usually used whole or coarsely chopped. Although some recipes require you to rinse them before use, for fast cooking I never bother with this. The beans will keep indefinitely if stored in a sealed jar in the refrigerator or in a cool place.

CHINESE WHITE CABBAGE OR BOK CHOY

Chinese white cabbage, more popularly known as bok choy, has been grown in China for centuries. Although there are many varieties, the most common and best-known is the one with a long, smooth, milky-white stem and large, crinkly, dark green leaves. The size of the plant indicates how tender it is; the smaller the better, especially in summer, when the hot weather toughens the stalks. It has a light, fresh, slightly mustardy taste and requires little cooking. Bok choy cooks quickly in soup and takes only minutes to stir-fry – perfect for fast cooking. It is now widely available in supermarkets. Look for firm crisp stalks and unblemished leaves. Store it in the bottom of the refrigerator.

CHILLIES

Fresh chillies – the seed pods of the capsicum plant – are used extensively in Chinese cookery. Although a relatively new ingredient, having been introduced from the Americas about 100 years ago, the chilli has spread rapidly throughout Asia. Chillies are becoming more and more easily available in the UK in supermarkets and specialist food shops. Although seldom used in traditional Cantonese cooking, they are ideal for flavouring food. They provide colour and form when used as a garnish, and are also added, chopped, to many dishes and sauces that require fast cooking. They are available fresh, dried or ground.

Fresh chillies Fresh chillies found in China are long and usually pointed. Both red and green are available, though you might have difficulty obtaining fresh red chillies in the UK. Their taste is mildly spicy and pungent. Smaller varieties can be found, but the larger longer ones are the most widely available. Look for fresh chillies that are bright in colour, with no brown patches or black spots. Use red chillies if possible as they are generally milder than green ones, because they sweeten as they ripen.

To prepare fresh chillies, first rinse them in cold water. Then, using a small sharp knife, slit them lengthways. Remove and discard the seeds. Rinse the chillies well under cold running water and prepare them according to the instructions in the recipe. Wash your hands, knife and chopping board before preparing other foods, and be careful not to touch your eyes until you have washed your hands thoroughly with soap and water.

<u>Dried red chillies</u> Although dried red chillies are associated with Sichuan-inspired dishes, they add dimension to many other types of cuisine. Some are small, thin and about ½ inch (1 cm) long. They are used to season oil for stir-fried dishes, or split and used in sauces or in braised dishes. They are normally left whole or cut in half lengthways and the seeds left in. Dried chillies can be bought at most supermarkets and Asian grocers', and they will keep indefinitely in a tightly covered jar in a cool place.

<u>Chilli bean sauce</u> *see* Thick Sauces and Pastes

<u>Chilli powder</u> Chilli powder, made from dried red chillies, is also known as cayenne pepper. It is pungent and aromatic, ranging from hot to very hot; it is thus widely used in many spicy dishes. You can buy it in supermarkets.

COCONUT MILK

Widely used throughout Asia, coconut milk is more important than cow's milk in the cooking of the region. It has some of the properties of cow's milk: the cream rises to the top when it is left to stand; it must be stirred as it comes to the boil; and the fat is chemically closer to butterfat than to vegetable fat. Coconut milk is not the liquid inside the coconut but the liquid 'wrung' from the grated and soaked flesh. It can be bought frozen or in tins. Both are of good quality and perfect for quick and easy cooking. For the purposes of this book, I recommend the tinned coconut milk which I have found quite acceptable and which certainly involves much less work than preparing your own. Look for the brands from Thailand or Malaysia: you can find these at Asian grocers', usually sold in 14 or 15 fl oz (380 or 400 ml) tins. Be sure to shake the tin well before opening. Place any left-over coconut milk in a covered glass jar and store in the refrigerator, where it will keep for a week.

CORIANDER, CHINESE PARSLEY OR CILANTRO

Fresh coriander is one of the relatively few herbs used in Chinese cookery. It is popular throughout southern China. It looks like flat parsley but its pungent, musky, citrus-like flavour gives it a distinctive character which is unmistakable. The feathery leaves are often used as a garnish; or the herb is chopped and mixed into sauces and stuffings. You can obtain it in many supermarkets now. When buying fresh coriander, look for deep green, fresh-looking leaves. Yellow and limp leaves indicate age and should be avoided.

To store coriander, wash it in cold water, drain it thoroughly or spin dry in a salad spinner and put it in a clean plastic bag with a couple of sheets of moist kitchen paper. I learned this technique from my cooking associate, Gordon Wing, and it works wonderfully. Stored in the salad compartment of your refrigerator, it will keep for several days.

CORNFLOUR

In China and Asia many different flours and types of starch, such as waterchestnut powder, taro starch and arrowroot, are used to bind and thicken sauces and to make batter. Traditional cooks used a bean flour because it thickened faster and held longer. Cornflour can help make quick sauces that are light and which barely coat the food so that it is never swimming in thick sauce. Added to a marinade, cornflour helps it to coat the food properly and gives the finished dish a velvety texture. It also protects food during deep-frying by helping to seal in the juices and produces a crisper coating than flour. It is used as a binder for minced stuffings too. When using cornflour in a sauce, first blend it with cold water until it forms a smooth paste and add it to the sauce at the last moment. It will look milky at first, but as the sauce cooks and thickens it turns clear and shiny.

CURRY PASTE

Curry flavours have been widely adopted by Chinese cooks. However, the Chinese like to use them more in the French style, achieving the fragrant aroma of curry but avoiding the overwhelming pungent spiciness which the Indians and Thais prefer. The most frequently used curry flavouring takes the form of prepared paste in which spices are mixed with oil and chillies. It has a better taste than the powdered variety. Be sure to get the Indian curry paste, often labelled 'Madras', which is generally the best. You can find it at some supermarkets and at many Chinese grocers'. If stored in the refrigerator after opening, curry paste keeps indefinitely.

FIVE-SPICE POWDER

Five-spice powder, also known as five-flavoured powder and five-fragrance spice powder, is available from many supermarkets (in the spice section) and Chinese grocers'. In Hong Kong Chinese chefs use this traditional spice in innovative ways, such as in marinating the inside of a Peking duck. It is a brownish powder consisting of a mixture of star anise, Sichuan peppercorns, fennel, cloves and cinnamon. A good blend is pungent, fragrant, spicy and slightly sweet at the same time. The exotic fragrance it gives to a dish makes the search for a good mixture well worth the effort. Stored in a well-sealed jar it keeps indefinitely.

FUNGUS

see Mushrooms, Chinese Dried

GARLIC

The pungent flavour of garlic is part of the fabric of Chinese cuisine. It would be inconceivable to cook without its distinctive, highly aromatic smell and unique taste. It is used in numerous ways: whole, finely chopped, crushed and pickled; and in Hong Kong I have even found it smoked. Garlic is used to flavour oils as well as spicy sauces, and is often paired with other equally pungent ingredients such as spring onions, black beans, curry paste, shrimp paste or fresh root ginger. For quick and easy preparation, give the garlic clove a sharp blow with the flat side of your cleaver or knife and the peel should come off easily. Then put the required amount through a garlic press, rather than chopping it in the traditional way – this saves time and works just as well.

Select fresh garlic which is firm and heavy, the cloves preferably pinkish in colour. It should be stored in a cool, dry place, but not in the refrigerator where it can easily become mildewed or begin to sprout.

GINGER

Fresh root ginger (actually a rhizome, not a root) in traditional Cantonese cooking is as ancient, traditional and essential as the wok. It is said that ginger from Canton is the most aromatic. Like garlic it is an indispensable ingredient of Chinese cookery. Its pungent, spicy and fresh taste adds a subtle but distinctive flavour to soups, meats, fish, sauces and vegetables. Ripe ginger is golden-beige in colour with a thin dry skin which is usually peeled before the ginger is used. It varies in size from small pieces to large knobbly 'hands'. Older shrivelled ginger is used for medicinal broths. Fresh ginger can now be found at many supermarkets and most Chinese grocers' shops. Look for 'roots' which are firm, solid and unmarked, with no signs of shrivelling. If wrapped in cling film, they will keep in the refrigerator for up to two weeks. Peeled ginger stored in a glass jar and covered in rice wine or dry sherry will last for several months. This has the added benefit of producing a flavoured wine that can be used in cooking.

Young ginger sometimes makes its appearance in Chinese grocers' shops. It is hard to find but well worth the search. Knobbly in shape and pink in colour, looking rather unformed, it is the newest spring growth of the plant. Young ginger is usually stir-fried as part of a recipe; in China it is commonly pickled. Because it is young and tender it does not need peeling and can be eaten as a vegetable. A popular way to eat pickled young ginger is with preserved 'thousand-year-old' duck eggs as a snack; it is also often served as an hors d'oeuvre.

MANGE-TOUT

This familiar vegetable combines a tender crisp texture and a sweet fresh flavour and cooks quickly. It is perhaps best when simply stir-fried with a little oil and salt and pieces of garlic and ginger. Frequently mange-tout are combined with meats. They are readily available from supermarkets and many greengrocers. Look for pods that are firm with very small peas, which means they are tender and young. They keep for at least a week, loosely wrapped, in the salad compartment of the refrigerator.

MUSHROOMS, CHINESE DRIED

There are many grades of these wonderful mushrooms said to have been produced for more than 1000 years in southern China. Black or brown in colour, they add a particular flavour and aroma to Chinese dishes. The best are very large ones with a lighter colour and a highly cracked surface; they are usually the most expensive. As you may imagine, they are very popular in Chinese cookery. Dried food shops in China carry all grades heaped in mounds, with the more expensive grades elaborately boxed. Outside China they can be bought from Chinese grocers' in boxes or plastic bags. Chinese dried mushrooms are expensive but a little goes a long way. Keep them stored in an air-tight jar in a cool dry place. Fresh ones (popularly known as Shiitake mushrooms – a Japanese term) are not an adequate substitute; the Chinese never use them fresh, preferring their distinct, robust, smoky flavour and yielding texture when dried. They are used chopped and combined with meats, fish and shellfish. They are well worth the relatively short time it takes to prepare them as they add a rich flavour to food.

To use Chinese dried mushrooms, soak the mushrooms in a bowl of warm water for about 20 minutes or until they are soft and pliable. Squeeze out the excess water and cut off and discard the woody stems. Only the caps are used.

The soaking water can be saved and used in soups or for cooking rice. Strain through a fine sieve to discard any sand or residue from the dried mushrooms. Dried mushrooms are particularly useful if you are in a hurry and do not have time to make a stock. Their presence will cover a multitude of omissions.

NOODLES/PASTA

In China you will see people eating noodles of all kinds, day and night, in restaurants and at food stalls. They provide a nutritious, quick, light snack and are usually of good quality. There are several styles of noodles which are ideal for quick and easy cooking – for example, the fresh thin egg noodles which are browned on both sides. Thin rice noodles are much savoured also, as are the fresh ones which are readily available in Chinese grocers' shops. Below is a list of the major types of noodles (or pasta) that can be bought in this country.

<u>Wheat noodles and egg noodles</u> These are made from hard or soft wheat flour and water. If egg has been added, the noodles are usually labelled 'egg noodles'. They can be bought dried or fresh from Chinese grocers', many supermarkets and delicatessens. Flat noodles are usually used in soups and rounded noodles are best for stir-frying or pan-frying. The fresh ones can be frozen successfully if they are first well wrapped. Thaw them thoroughly before using.

Wheat and egg noodles are very good blanched and served with a main dish instead of plain rice. Dried wheat or fresh egg noodles are best. Allow 4 oz (110 g) fresh or dried Chinese egg or wheat noodles per person. To prepare fresh noodles, immerse them in a pan of boiling water and cook for 3–5 minutes or until done to your taste. To prepare dried noodles, cook either according to the instructions on the packet or in boiling water for 4–5 minutes. Then drain and serve.

If you are cooking noodles some time in advance of serving them or before stir-frying them, toss the cooked drained noodles in 2 teaspoons sesame oil and put them into a bowl. Cover this with cling film and refrigerate. The cooked noodles will remain useable for about 2 hours.

<u>Rice noodles</u> Rice noodles are popular in southern China. I find them a great convenience as, being dried, they do not need refrigeration and are quickly prepared for a fast meal. They are available from Chinese grocers' and are sometimes called 'rice stick noodles'. They are flat and about the length of a chopstick. They can also vary in thickness: use the type called for in the recipe. Rice noodles are very easy to use and inexpensive. Simply soak them in warm water for 20 minutes or until they are soft. Drain them in a colander or sieve and then use in soups or stir-fried dishes.

<u>Bean thread (transparent) noodles</u> These, also called cellophane noodles, are made not from a grain flour but from ground mung beans. They are available dried, and are very fine and white. Easy to recognise, packed in their neat plastic-wrapped bundles, they are stocked by most Chinese grocers' and some supermarkets. They are never served on their own, but are added to soups or braised dishes or are deep-fried and used as a garnish – they are suitable for a quick meal. They must be soaked in warm water for about 5 minutes before use. As they are rather long, you might find it easier to cut them into shorter lengths after soaking. If you intend to fry them, they need first to be separated. They are quite brittle so a good technique is to separate the strands within a large paper bag to keep them from flying all over the place. If you are going to fry them, do not soak them before use.

OILS

Oil is the most commonly used cooking medium in Chinese cuisine and the favourite is groundnut (peanut) oil. Animal fats, usually lard and chicken fat, are also used in some areas. I prefer to cook with groundnut oil as I find animal fats in general too heavy.

Oil can often be re-used after frying. When this is possible, simply allow the oil to cool after use and filter it through cheesecloth or a fine-meshed sieve into a jar. Cover it tightly and store in a cool dry place. If you keep it in the refrigerator it will become cloudy but it will clarify again when it returns to room temperature. From the point of view of flavour I find that it is best to re-use oil no more than once, and this is healthier since constantly re-used oils increase in saturated fat content. However, for real clarity of flavour I prefer *not* to re-use oil at all; I think that oil should be *always* fresh as this helps achieve consistently high-quality results in cooking.

Groundnut oil Also known as peanut oil, this is the preferred oil in Chinese cookery because it has a pleasant, mild, unobtrusive taste. Its ability to be heated to a high temperature without burning makes it perfect for stir-frying and deep-frying. The groundnut oils found in China are cold-pressed and have the fragrance of freshly roasted peanuts. Some Chinese supermarkets stock the Hong Kong brands, labelled in Chinese only; these are well worth searching for. But if you cannot find them, use groundnut oil from your local supermarket.

Corn oil Corn oil is a healthful, mostly polyunsaturated oil that is good for cooking, particularly deep-frying, as it can be heated to a high temperature without burning. However, I find it rather heavy with a noticeable smell and taste.

Other vegetable oils Some of the cheaper vegetable oils available include soya bean, safflower and sunflower. They are light in colour and taste and can also be used in cooking.

Sesame Oil This thick, rich, golden-brown or dark-coloured oil is made from roasted sesame seeds, and has a distinctive nutty flavour and aroma. It is widely used in Chinese cooking in limited amounts in marinades or as a final seasoning – it is added at the end of cooking to enrich a dish subtly without overcoming its basic flavour. It is not normally used as a cooking oil with other oils except in northern China. It is sold in bottles by many supermarkets and Chinese grocers'.

OYSTER SAUCE

This is one of my favourite sauces for quick cooking. It is easy to make a delicious sauce in no time at all using oyster sauce, which gives a rich aroma to a dish. Thick and brown, it is made from a concentrate of oysters cooked in soy sauce, seasonings and brine. Despite its name, oyster sauce does not taste fishy. It has a rich flavour and is used not only in cooking but also as a condiment, diluted with a little oil, for vegetables, poultry or meat; it is very versatile. It is usually sold in bottles and can be bought in Chinese grocers' shops and some supermarkets. Look for the most expensive brands as they are the highest in quality. Keep refrigerated after opening.

RICE

Long-grain rice This is the most popular rice for cooking in southern China. The Chinese go through the ritual of washing it, but in the case of rice purchased at a supermarket, this step can be omitted for quick cookery. One of my favourite rices is the long-grain variety from Thailand which has a pleasing fragrance, like that of the Indian basmati rice. Thai aromatic long-grain rice is now available from many Chinese and Southeast Asian grocers'.

Short-grain rice Short-grain rice is not as frequently used in Chinese cooking as the long-grain type except for making morning rice porridge. It is more popular in Japan. Suitable brands which can be found in many Chinese or Japanese food shops are known as 'American Rose' or 'Japanese Rose'. Short-grain rice is slightly stickier than long-grain white rice.

RICE WINE, CHINESE

An important contributor to the flavour of Chinese cuisine, this wine is used extensively for cooking and drinking throughout the country. There are many varieties but the finest is believed to be that from Shaoxing in Zhejiang Province in eastern China. It is made from glutinous rice, yeast and spring water. Chefs frequently use rice wine not only for cooking but also in marinades. It is now readily available from Chinese grocers' and some wine merchants. Store it, tightly corked, at room temperature. A good-quality, pale, dry sherry can be substituted for Chinese rice wine but cannot equal its rich mellow taste. Do not confuse this wine with *sake*, which is the Japanese version of rice wine and quite different. Western grape wines are not an adequate substitute either.

THICK SAUCES AND PASTES

Quick and easy Chinese cookery involves the use of a number of thick tasty sauces and pastes. These are essential to the authentic taste of the food and it is well worth making the effort to obtain them. Most are now easy to find; they are sold in bottles or tins by Chinese food shops and some supermarkets. Tinned sauces, once opened, should be transferred to screw-top glass jars and kept in the refrigerator where they will last indefinitely. Using these sauces in your cooking produces delicious results with little effort.

Bean sauce This thick, spicy, aromatic sauce is made with yellow beans, flour and salt which are fermented together. It is quite salty but adds a distinctive flavour to sauces and is frequently used in Chinese cookery. There are two forms: whole beans in a thick sauce; and mashed or puréed beans (sold as 'crushed yellow bean sauce'). I prefer the whole bean variety because it is slightly less salty and has a better texture. It keeps indefinitely in the refrigerator.

Chilli bean sauce This thick, dark sauce or paste, made from soya beans, chillies and other seasonings, is very hot and spicy. Formerly used in cooking only in western China, it is now widely used throughout the country and is usually available here in jars. Be sure to seal the jar tightly after use and store in the refrigerator. Do not confuse chilli bean sauce with chilli sauce which is hot, red, thinner and made without beans and is used mainly as a dipping sauce for cooked dishes. There are Southeast Asian versions of chilli bean sauce (called *sate* sauce) which I find very spicy and hot. You can use them as a substitute for chilli bean sauce if you like really spicy food.

Hoisin sauce Widely used in this book, this thick, dark, brownish red sauce is made from soya beans, vinegar, sugar, spices and other flavourings. Sweet and spicy, it is a very popular ingredient in southern Chinese cookery. In the West it is often used as a sauce for Peking duck instead of the traditional sweet bean sauce. Hoisin sauce (sometimes also labelled 'barbecue sauce') is sold in tins and jars. When refrigerated, it keeps indefinitely.

<u>Sesame paste</u> This rich, thick, creamy brown paste is made from roasted sesame seeds, unlike the Middle Eastern *tahini*. It is sold in jars by Chinese food shops. If oil has separated from the paste in the jar, empty the contents into a blender or food processor and mix well. Chinese sesame paste is used in both hot and cold dishes and is particularly popular in northern and western China. If you cannot obtain it, use a smooth peanut butter instead.

SHALLOTS

Shallots are mild-flavoured members of the onion family. They are small – about the size of pickling onions – with copper-red skins and should be peeled before use just like onions. They have a distinctive onion taste without being as strong or overpowering as ordinary onions, and I think they are an excellent substitute for Chinese shallots which can sometimes be bought from Chinese grocers'. Buy shallots at supermarkets and keep them in a cool dry place (not the refrigerator).

SOY SAUCES

Soy sauce is an essential ingredient in Chinese cooking. It is made from a mixture of soya beans, flour and water which is then naturally fermented and aged for some months. The distilled liquid is soy sauce. New versions containing less salt are now available. There are two main types:

<u>Light soy sauce</u> As the name implies, this is light in colour, but it is full of flavour and is the best one to use for cooking. It is saltier than dark soy sauce. It is known in Chinese grocers' shops as Superior Soy. This type of soy sauce was used extensively for testing the recipes in this book.

<u>Dark soy sauce</u> This sauce is aged for much longer than light soy sauce, hence its darker, almost black colour. It is slightly thicker and stronger than light soy sauce and is more suitable for stews. I prefer it to light soy as a dipping sauce. It is known in Chinese grocers' shops as Soy Superior Sauce, and although used less frequently it is nevertheless important to have on hand.

SUGAR

Sugar has, appropriately, been used sparingly in the cooking of savoury dishes in China for 1000 years. Properly employed, it helps balance the various flavours of sauces and other dishes. Chinese sugar comes in several forms: as rock or yellow lump sugar, as brown sugar slabs, and as maltose or malt sugar. I particularly like to use rock sugar which is rich and has a more subtle flavour than that of refined granulated sugar. It also gives a good lustre or glaze to braised dishes and sauces. You can buy it in Chinese food shops, where it is usually sold in packets. You may need to break the lumps into smaller pieces with a wooden mallet or rolling pin. If you cannot find it, use white sugar or coffee sugar crystals (the amber, chunky kind) instead. For fast cooking, use white granulated sugar.

VINEGARS

Vinegars are widely used in China as dipping sauces as well as for cooking. Unlike Western vinegars, they are usually made from rice. There are many varieties, ranging in flavour from the spicy and slightly tart to the sweet and pungent. Experiment with them. They keep indefinitely.

White rice vinegar White rice vinegar is clear and mild in flavour. It has a faint taste of glutinous rice and is used for sweet and sour dishes.

STARTERS & APPETISERS

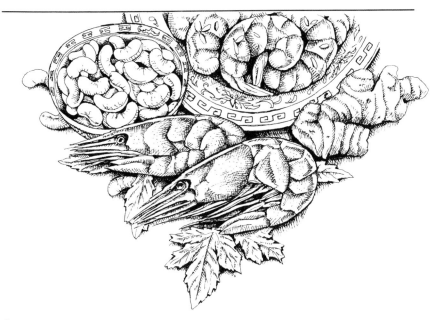

*I*t may seem a contradiction in terms to have starters in a 'quick and easy' cookbook, but there is a place for them – so long as they *are* quick and easy. These recipes fit that description, being simple but delicious. The cooking techniques include grilling, stir-frying or deep-frying – and some of the dishes involve no cooking at all! When time is a factor in the preparation of a meal, I prefer starters that can be made in advance and then finished at the last moment, quickly and easily.

Remember, too, that these very same dishes can be prepared as part of a more elaborate meal when you have more time at your disposal. Alternatively, you could serve some of the main course dishes in smaller quantities as starters. It is nice to have different tastes and textures within one meal. The reasoning behind this cookbook is that 'quick and easy' should mean 'pleasing and delicious'.

GRILLED PRAWNS WITH FRESH CORIANDER AND GINGER SAUCE

*P*rawns make a wonderful starter because they are easy to prepare and are popular with most people. They may seem expensive but a little goes a long way and they certainly whet the appetite. Most of the work in this recipe may be done well in advance – the actual cooking takes but 5 minutes and the shellfish emerge from under the grill redolent of the fresh coriander and tangy ginger, an ideal appetiser for guests.

These prawns cook wonderfully on a barbecue but I have found that they are just as tasty when grilled, so if the weather turns inclement, you can move indoors and still enjoy them. If you plan a larger gathering, the quantities given in the recipe may be increased several times with no loss of delectation. Moreover, these prawns may serve as an elegant cold buffet dish or, if you wish, as a quick and easy lunch.

SHOPPING LIST
> *1 lb (450 g) fresh uncooked prawns*
> *Fresh root ginger*
> *Fresh coriander*

PREPARATION TIME *30 minutes*

COOKING TIME *5 minutes*

SERVES 2–4

1 lb (450 g) fresh uncooked prawns

For the marinade
1 tablespoon light soy sauce
1 teaspoon Chinese rice wine or dry sherry
1 teaspoon sesame oil

For the sauce
2 tablespoons finely chopped fresh coriander
2 teaspoons white rice vinegar
1 teaspoon finely chopped fresh root ginger

Pre-heat the grill or prepare the barbecue.

Peel the prawns and discard the shells. Using a small sharp knife, partially split the prawns lengthways and remove the fine digestive cord – if you are particularly short of time you can omit this stage. Pat the prawns dry with kitchen paper.

Combine the marinade ingredients, add the prawns and set aside for 10 minutes. Prepare the sauce ingredients, mix them together and set aside.

Lay the prawns on a baking tray big enough to fit under the grill. Alternatively, cook them on the barbecue, weather permitting. Cook the prawns for 3 minutes on one side, turn over and cook for 2 minutes on the other side.

Turn the prawns on to a serving platter and serve with the sauce.

CHINESE BARBECUED CHICKEN WINGS

Chinese cuisine offers some of the most delicious and stimulating barbecue sauces. Of course, I might be biased on the matter! There can be little doubt, however, that the sauces are easy to prepare. I like to use this combination of sauces with chicken wings, a cheap and humble food that is thereby transformed into a delightful dish. If you wish, you can substitute chicken breasts, but cook them for less time. Serve these tasty morsels with drinks; the quantities given below are for a large group, but for an even bigger gathering simply double or triple the ingredients. The chicken wings take a few minutes to cook but need no watching and you can, meanwhile, be about other things. Serve them hot or let them cool to room temperature; they are quite as wonderful after they have cooled and thus make a most appropriate picnic dish.

If it helps your schedule, you can prepare the wings and sauce on the morning of the day you intend to cook them. Leave them covered with cling film in the refrigerator, but be sure to bring them to room temperature before cooking. As a further time saver, make a double batch of barbecue sauce and use half of it later in the week to accompany grilled lamb or pork chops.

SHOPPING LIST
  2 lb (900 g) chicken wings
  Garlic
  Fresh root ginger

PREPARATION TIME *10 minutes*

COOKING TIME *35 minutes*

SERVES 4

2 lb (900 g) chicken wings

For the barbecue sauce
2 tablespoons dark soy sauce
3 tablespoons hoisin sauce
2 large cloves garlic, peeled
1 tablespoon coarsely chopped
  fresh root ginger
1 tablespoon Chinese rice wine
  or dry sherry
1 tablespoon sesame oil
2 teaspoons chilli bean sauce
2 teaspoons sugar

Pre-heat the oven to gas mark 9, 475°F (240°C).

Place the chicken wings in an ovenproof baking dish.

Combine the barbecue sauce ingredients in a blender and mix for 5 seconds. Add the sauce to the chicken wings and toss to coat thoroughly. Place the wings in the oven and cook for 15 minutes. Turn the heat down to gas mark 4, 350°F (180°C) and cook for a further 20 minutes. Serve hot or allow to cool and serve at room temperature.

MINCED PRAWNS WITH LETTUCE CUPS

*T*his elegant dish is derived from a more sumptuous one that uses lobster as its main ingredient. No matter; prawns are a perfectly acceptable substitute. In fact, prawns are ideal for quick and easy meals because they need only a short cooking time – in this case 5–6 minutes. It is a colourful dish with contrasting textures and makes an impressive starter for any meal; but it may also serve as a refreshing light lunch. Other vegetables in season, such as carrots or courgettes, may be substituted for the red peppers or asparagus and cooked in the same way.

SHOPPING LIST

> *1 lb (450 g) Iceberg lettuce*
> *8 oz (225 g) fresh uncooked*
> *prawns*
> *8 oz (225 g) red peppers*
> *4 oz (110 g) asparagus*
> *Garlic*
> *Fresh root ginger*
> *Spring onions*

PREPARATION TIME *15–20 minutes*

COOKING TIME *5–6 minutes*

SERVES 4

1 lb (450 g) Iceberg lettuce
8 oz (225 g) fresh uncooked
  prawns
8 oz (225 g) red peppers
4 oz (110 g) asparagus
1½ tablespoons oil (preferably
  groundnut)
2 tablespoons coarsely chopped
  garlic
2 tablespoons coarsely chopped
  fresh root ginger
4 tablespoons coarsely chopped
  spring onions
1 teaspoon salt
2 teaspoons light soy sauce
2 teaspoons sesame oil
4 tablespoons hoisin sauce

Separate, wash and dry the lettuce leaves.

Peel the prawns and discard the shells. Using a small sharp knife, partially split the prawns lengthways and remove the fine digestive cord – if you are particularly short of time you can omit this stage. Pat the prawns dry with kitchen paper and coarsely chop them.

Finely dice the peppers and asparagus and set aside.

Heat a wok or large frying-pan and add the oil. Add the garlic, ginger and spring onions and stir-fry for 10 seconds. Put in the vegetables and continue to stir-fry for 3 minutes. Add the prawns, salt, soy sauce and sesame oil and continue to cook for 2 minutes. Turn the mixture on to a serving plate. Arrange the lettuce on a separate plate, put the hoisin sauce in a small bowl and serve. Each guest puts a heap of each ingredient on a lettuce leaf, wraps it up and eats it with the fingers.

COLD CUCUMBER SALAD

*H*ere is a really quick and easy recipe in which you salt the cucumbers and 'sweat' the moisture from them for 15 minutes. They acquire a 'cooked' texture without cooking and make a charming starter. They can also serve as a picnic dish or as part of a summer salad. Garnish with blanched red pepper strips, if you wish to add a note of colour.

SHOPPING LIST
: *1 lb (450 g) cucumbers*
1 large shallot
Garlic
1 fresh red chilli

PREPARATION TIME *30 minutes*

COOKING TIME *None*

SERVES 4–6

1 lb (450 g) cucumbers
2 teaspoons salt

For the sauce
1 tablespoon finely chopped shallots
2 teaspoons finely chopped garlic
1 teaspoon light soy sauce
1 teaspoon dark soy sauce
2 tablespoons white rice vinegar
2 teaspoons sugar
1 small fresh red chilli, finely chopped
1 tablespoon sesame oil

For the garnish
Blanched red pepper strips

Peel the cucumbers and slice them in half lengthways. Using a teaspoon, remove the seeds. Cut the cucumber halves into 3 × ½ inch (7.5 × 1 cm) pieces and put them into a colander set inside a bowl. Sprinkle the pieces with the salt, mix well and set aside for 15 minutes.

Next combine the sauce ingredients thoroughly in a small bowl and set aside.

Rinse the cucumber pieces, pat them dry with kitchen paper and mix with the sauce. Let them marinate for 10 minutes, garnish with the red pepper strips (if using), then serve.

Spicy Fried Cashew Nuts

*M*any Hong Kong restaurants serve small platters of stir-fried or deep-fried peanuts with seasoned salt as an appetiser. I have always enjoyed them and believe that they should be part of everyone's repertoire of starters. Here I use cashews, my favourite nuts. Their flavour stands up very nicely to the robustness of the spices. Easily made in advance, they go well with drinks and can be served warm or cold.

SHOPPING LIST
8 oz (225 g) raw cashew nuts

PREPARATION TIME *8 minutes*

COOKING TIME *6 minutes*

MAKES 8 oz (225 g)

10 fl oz (300 ml) oil (preferably groundnut)
8 oz (225 g) raw cashew nuts
1 teaspoon salt
½ teaspoon freshly ground black pepper
½ teaspoon chilli powder
¼ teaspoon five-spice powder

Heat a wok or large frying-pan, then add the oil. When the oil begins to smoke lightly, deep-fry the cashew nuts for 2 minutes or until they begin to turn slightly brown. While the nuts are browning, start to heat another frying-pan. Remove the nuts from the oil with a slotted spoon – do not allow them to brown very deeply as they continue cooking after they have been taken out of the oil. Add the nuts directly to the hot frying-pan. Add the salt, pepper, chilli powder and five-spice powder and stir-fry for 2 minutes or until the cashew nuts are well coated with the spice. Allow to cool before serving with drinks.

CRISPY PRAWNS

During one of my many trips to Australia, Charmaine Solomon, an authority on Asian cuisines, introduced me to this dish. It is to be found in one of her delightfully written cookbooks and I unabashedly lift it and share it with you. The prawns are so good that they could serve as a main course, and they are so tasty that no dipping sauce is needed.

SHOPPING LIST
    1 lb (450 g) fresh uncooked
        prawns
    Breadcrumbs

PREPARATION TIME *25 minutes*

COOKING TIME *3–4 minutes*

SERVES 6–8 as a starter

    1 lb (450 g) fresh uncooked
    prawns

2 teaspoons light soy sauce
1 tablespoon Chinese rice wine
    or dry sherry
1 teaspoon five-spice powder
¼ teaspoon freshly ground
    black pepper
15 fl oz (400 ml) oil (preferably
    groundnut)
8 tablespoons cornflour
2 eggs, beaten
10 tablespoons breadcrumbs

Peel the prawns and discard the shells. Using a small sharp knife, partially split the prawns lengthways and remove the fine digestive cord – you can omit this stage. Pat the prawns dry with kitchen paper. Mix the prawns with the soy sauce, rice wine, five-spice powder and pepper.

Heat a wok or large deep frying-pan, then add the oil. While the oil is heating, dip the prawns in the cornflour, shaking them gently to remove any excess, then dip them into the beaten eggs and finally coat them thoroughly with the breadcrumbs. A clean and easy way to do this is to place the cornflour and the breadcrumbs in two separate polythene or paper bags. Toss the prawns gently in the first bag with the cornflour, remove them and put them in the bowl with the beaten eggs, making sure that they are well coated. Then transfer them with a slotted spoon to the bag containing the breadcrumbs and toss gently.

When the oil begins to smoke slightly, deep-fry the coated prawns for 3–4 minutes or until they are golden-brown. Drain them well on kitchen paper and serve at once.

2

SOUPS

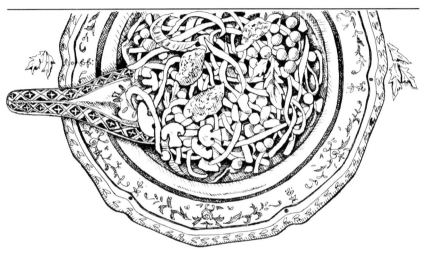

*S*oups cannot be made quickly and still taste as they should: you must use decent stock. Soup made with water is insipid – unless it is fish soup, in which case the assertive sea flavour enlivens the water. Preservatives and artificial flavourings keep me away from commercial tinned and cubed stocks. Thus this section proposes something of a compromise. Instead of the traditional long-simmering stock, I use a more quickly made stock which is nevertheless home-made and of very good quality, which matters even more when you are in a hurry. Once the stock is made and frozen, you have at hand the basis of quick and easy soups.

QUICK AND EASY CHICKEN STOCK

*T*here is no comparison between stock made from scratch and the commercially available kind. Even if you are normally pressed for time, do make the opportunity to prepare this stock in advance for soups that will then be quick and easy and delicious. Twenty minutes of work and an hour of simmering is all that you need here. Freeze the stock and you have prepared the foundation for real soup.

I use chicken wings because they are fast-cooking, cheap and have a good flavour.

SHOPPING LIST
2 lb (900 g) chicken wings
Fresh root ginger
Spring onions
Garlic

PREPARATION TIME *20 minutes*

COOKING TIME *1 hour*

MAKES 2 pints (1.1 litres)

2 lb (900 g) chicken wings
2½ pints (1.4 litres) water
3 slices fresh root ginger
4 spring onions
2 large cloves garlic
2 teaspoons salt

Put the chicken wings into a large saucepan. Cover with the water and bring to simmering point.

Meanwhile, cut the ginger into diagonal slices 2 × ½ inch (5 ×1 cm). Discard the green tops from the spring onions and cut the remainder into thirds. Lightly crush the garlic cloves, leaving the skins on.

As the water in the pan begins to simmer, gently skim off the scum as it rises to the surface using a large flat spoon. Add the spring onions, ginger, garlic and salt and partially cover. Gently simmer for 1 hour.

Strain the stock through a fine-meshed sieve. Remove any surface fat. It is now ready for use or it can be allowed to cool thoroughly before being transferred to containers and frozen for future use.

Cold Cucumber Salad (page 28)
Grilled Prawns with Fresh Coriander and Ginger Sauce (page 24)

RICH BEEF SOUP

*T*his satisfying savoury soup is perfect for those who like to make a meal of soup and salad. The beef is minced and thus cooks faster than slices or chunks would; the seasonings give it added dimension. The soup re-heats very well and can be prepared in advance. It takes 25 minutes from kitchen to table.

SHOPPING LIST
> *8 oz (225 g) minced beef*
> *2 eggs*
> *Spring onions*

PREPARATION TIME *15 minutes*

COOKING TIME *7 minutes*

SERVES 4–6

> 8 oz (225 g) minced beef
> 1 tablespoon plus 2 teaspoons
>   dark soy sauce

2 teaspoons Chinese rice wine
  or dry sherry
1 teaspoon plus 1 tablespoon
  cornflour
2 pints (1.1 litres) Chicken
  Stock (see page 32)
1 teaspoon chilli bean sauce
½ teaspoon freshly ground
  white or black pepper
2 eggs, beaten
4 tablespoons coarsely chopped
  spring onions

Combine the beef with 1 tablespoon of the soy sauce, the rice wine and 1 teaspoon of the cornflour. Mix the remaining 1 tablespoon cornflour with 1 tablespoon water.

Put the stock into a saucepan and bring to simmering point. Add the beef and the cornflour-and-water mixture, and stir for 1 minute, breaking up any clumps of meat. Then add the remaining 2 teaspoons soy sauce, the chilli bean sauce and pepper. Simmer for 2 minutes. Stir in the beaten eggs and finally garnish with the chopped spring onions. Serve at once.

Chicken with Rice Noodles in Soup (page 36)
Rich Beef Soup (page 35)

CHICKEN WITH RICE NOODLES IN SOUP

With your stock ready-made and waiting in the freezer, this is quick and easy to prepare. It is comforting, satisfying real food, perfect for a cold winter's day when you do not have time for involved shopping and the pickings are slim because of the weather. It is both filling and light at the same time. Add other vegetables for a more substantial meal – mange-tout are perfect and need only be trimmed before being blanched in the hot stock. If you like spicy soup, as I do, stir in a teaspoon or two of chilli bean sauce and perhaps 1½ teaspoons lemon or lime juice.

SHOPPING LIST
> *4 oz (110 g) boneless chicken*
> *breast*
> *Spring onions*

PREPARATION TIME *5 minutes*

COOKING TIME *10 minutes*

SERVES 4–6

2 pints (1.1 litres) Chicken
Stock (see page 32)
4 oz (110 g) boneless chicken
breast
4 oz (110 g) dried rice noodles
1 teaspoon salt
2 teaspoons sesame oil
2 finely chopped spring onions
to garnish

Bring the chicken stock to a simmer. Finely shred the chicken breast. Add the chicken and rice noodles to the stock and simmer for 5 minutes or until the chicken is just cooked through. Add salt and sesame oil, sprinkle the spring onions over the top and serve at once.

CHICKEN AND WATERCRESS SOUP

I was fortunate to have a mother who was a good cook. Because she worked out of the home, however, she by necessity made an art of quick and easy meals, especially soups. This delectable Chicken-Watercress soup was a family favourite. The mushrooms add substance as well as an earthy flavour, but if you are really in a hurry they may be omitted. I highly recommend that you include them, however: the few minutes' extra time is well worth it. If you like, you can substitute spinach for the watercress.

SHOPPING LIST
12 oz (350 g) boneless chicken
breasts
8 oz (225 g) watercress

PREPARATION TIME *12 minutes*

COOKING TIME *12 minutes*

SERVES 4–6

½ oz (10 g) dried Chinese
  mushrooms
12 oz (350 g) boneless chicken
  breasts
1½ teaspoons salt
1 teaspoon Chinese rice wine or
  dry sherry
1 teaspoon cornflour
8 oz (225 g) watercress
2 pints (1.1 litres) Chicken
  Stock (see page 32)
2 teaspoons sesame oil

Soak the dried Chinese mushrooms in warm water for about 15 minutes. Meanwhile, shred the chicken breasts and combine them with ½ teaspoon of the salt, the rice wine and cornflour. Wash the watercress, discarding any tough stems.

Put the stock into a saucepan and bring to simmering point. While the stock is heating, remove the mushrooms from their water and squeeze out any excess liquid. Cut off the stalks and discard them. Add the mushrooms to the simmering stock and continue to cook for 5 minutes. Now add the chicken and watercress, turn off the heat and add the remaining 1 teaspoon salt and the sesame oil. Give the soup several stirs and allow it to stand for 2 minutes before serving.

TOMATO GINGER SOUP

*T*his soup is a year-round favourite of mine because it can be made successfully with tinned tomatoes, one of the few processed foods I find acceptable, and so need not wait for fresh tomatoes to come into season. Of course, it is delicious made with fresh ripe tomatoes when they are available at a reasonable price, and they also need little preparation and cook quickly. This is a refreshing soup which makes a sparkling starter. On hot summer days, try serving it at room temperature. For a Southeast Asian touch, add 2 tablespoons lemon juice. The soup re-heats successfully.

SHOPPING LIST
1 lb (450 g) fresh or tinned
tomatoes
Fresh root ginger

PREPARATION TIME *9 minutes*

COOKING TIME *6 minutes*

SERVES 4–6

1 lb (450 g) fresh or tinned
tomatoes
2 pints (1.1 litres) Chicken
Stock (see page 32)
3 tablespoons coarsely chopped
fresh root ginger
1 tablespoon light soy sauce
2 teaspoons chilli bean sauce
2 teaspoons sugar

If you are using fresh tomatoes, cut them in half horizontally and squeeze out the seeds. Coarsely chop the flesh and set aside. If you are using tinned tomatoes, drain thoroughly and chop them roughly.

Put the stock into a saucepan and bring to simmering point. Add the ginger, soy sauce, chilli bean sauce, sugar and tomatoes. Simmer for 2 minutes. Serve at once.

FAST SEAFOOD SOUP

When you really don't have time, there is no stock in your freezer and you want a change of pace, do as some Chinese families do: use fish to make a quick seafood soup. The assertive flavour of the fish combined with rice wine and ginger provides a tasty base. For a soup redolent of the flavour of China, add clams or mussels and prawns. It is a light but nutritious soup.

SHOPPING LIST
1 lb (450 g) fresh fish fillets
(preferably cod or haddock)
Fresh root ginger

PREPARATION TIME *10 minutes*

COOKING TIME *10 minutes*

SERVES 4

1 lb (450 g) fresh fish fillets

1 teaspoon salt
½ teaspoon freshly ground
white or black pepper
2 teaspoons sesame oil
1 pint (570 ml) water
5 fl oz (150 ml) Chinese rice
wine or dry sherry
1 tablespoon finely chopped
fresh root ginger
1 tablespoon light soy sauce
1 teaspoon chilli bean sauce

Cut the fish fillets into 2 inch (5 cm) square pieces and mix with the salt, pepper and sesame oil.

Bring the water and rice wine to the boil, boil for 1 minute and then lower the heat until the liquid is just simmering. Add the ginger, soy sauce, chilli bean sauce and the fish chunks and simmer for 5 minutes or until the fish is just cooked through. Serve at once.

TRI-COLOUR SOUP

*P*erfect for a holiday or any other day, this colourful and appetising soup is as delicious and nutritious as it looks: refreshing, light and full of flavour. It makes a perfect starter and can double as a main dish for a quick family meal. Other vegetables in season, such as Chinese flowering cabbage, Chinese leaves or Swiss chard, may replace the spinach.

SHOPPING LIST
> *8 oz (225 g) fresh or tinned*
> *tomatoes*
> *8 oz (225 g) firm bean curd*
> *8 oz (225 g) fresh spinach*

PREPARATION TIME *17 minutes*

COOKING TIME *6 minutes*

SERVES 4–6

8 oz (225 g) fresh or tinned
  tomatoes
8 oz (225 g) firm bean curd
8 oz (225 g) fresh spinach
2 pints (1.1 litres) Chicken
  Stock (see page 32)
1 tablespoon light soy sauce
½ teaspoon freshly ground
  white or black pepper
½ teaspoon sugar
½ teaspoon white rice vinegar

If you are using fresh tomatoes, cut them in half horizontally and squeeze out the seeds. Coarsely chop the flesh and set aside. If you are using tinned tomatoes, drain and chop them roughly. Cut the bean curd into ½ inch (1 cm) pieces. Remove stalks from the spinach and wash leaves well.

Bring the stock to a simmer in a medium-sized saucepan. Add the tomatoes, bean curd and spinach, and simmer for 2 minutes. Then add the soy sauce, pepper, sugar and vinegar. Give the soup several gentle stirs and serve at once.

WHOLE FISH SOUP

*T*his elegant fish soup is taken from the menu of the Chiu Chow Garden restaurant in Hong Kong. I first tasted it there in the company of Jeff Smith, the 'Frugal Gourmet', and perhaps America's best-known television cook. It is a most impressive dish to serve when you are entertaining and are short of time to prepare food. A whole fish brings good luck, the Chinese say. What is certain is that it brings good taste to soup.

If you wish, you can serve the fish with a dipping sauce of soy sauce, chopped spring onions and finely sliced fresh root ginger, and serve the soup separately.

SHOPPING LIST
  1–1½ lb (450–700 g) fresh
    whole fish or 1 inch (2.5 cm)
    thick fish fillets (preferably
    sea bass, cod or haddock)
  Fresh root ginger
  8 oz (225 g) celery
  Spring onions

PREPARATION TIME *15 minutes*

COOKING TIME *10 minutes plus 10*
    minutes' standing time

SERVES 4–6

1–1½ lb (450–700 g) fresh
    whole fish or fillets
2½ pints (1.4 litres) water
1½ teaspoons salt
4 tablespoons finely shredded
    fresh root ginger
8 oz (225 g) celery, coarsely
    chopped
1 tablespoon light soy sauce
1 tablespoon Chinese rice wine
    or dry sherry
4 spring onions, shredded
1 tablespoon sesame oil

If you are using a whole fish, clean it and remove the gills. Either leave the head on as the Chinese do or remove it if you prefer. If you are using fish fillets, remove the skin. Wash the fish thoroughly. Using a sharp knife or cleaver, cut diagonal slices across either side of the whole fish or on one side of the fillets. Do not cut right through, but keep the fish or fillets intact.

Bring the water to a simmer and gently lower in the fish. Simmer for 2 minutes and add the rest of the ingredients except the sesame oil. Cover and simmer for another 8 minutes. Turn off the heat, then leave the soup to stand for 10 minutes. Just before serving, stir in the sesame oil.

3

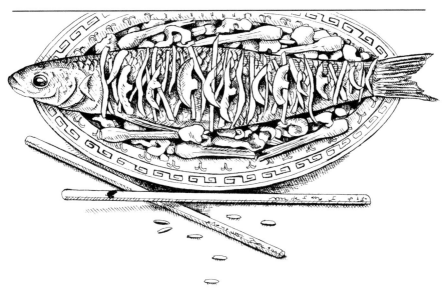

FISH & SEAFOOD

*F*ish and shellfish by their very nature are best when not overcooked. The sweet succulent sea flavours are retained through careful and quick cooking. Fish is thus most appropriate for the 'quick and easy' approach. First you must buy the freshest you can find; then you must cook it quickly and with the appropriate seasonings. I think that no other cuisine matches that of the Chinese in its ability to capture the best flavours and textures of the harvest of the sea. I draw upon that heritage for the recipes in this section.

Firm white fish such as cod, haddock and even plaice lend themselves best to the steaming technique. This delicate process gently brings out the virtues of the food. Chinese spices, such as black beans, can be used on more assertively flavoured fish and shellfish such as salmon and mussels. Ginger, garlic and spring onions are very congenial seasonings for all fish or seafood. Serve any of the following recipes with another vegetable dish and rice or potatoes and you have the best of contemporary dining, whether for entertaining a large party or for informal eating with family and friends.

QUICK PAN-FRIED FIVE-SPICE FISH

On the way home from work, my widowed mother would often pick up a small whole fish or some fillets and quickly put together this nutritious meal. With stir-fried vegetables, yesterday's rice re-heated and perhaps a Western touch of salad, you have a quick, wholesome and satisfying meal. The fish also goes wonderfully well with pasta. For a more elegant meal try substituting fresh uncooked prawns for the fish.

SHOPPING LIST

1 lb (450 g) fresh fish fillets
(preferably cod or haddock)
Garlic
Fresh root ginger

PREPARATION TIME *10 minutes*

COOKING TIME *10 minutes*

SERVES 4

1 lb (450 g) fresh fish fillets
1 teaspoon five-spice powder
1 teaspoon salt
1½ tablespoons oil (preferably groundnut)
2 tablespoons coarsely chopped garlic
2 tablespoons coarsely chopped fresh root ginger
1½ tablespoons Chinese rice wine or dry sherry
2 teaspoons light soy sauce
2 teaspoons sesame oil

Rub the fish fillets with the five-spice powder and salt.

Heat a wok or large frying-pan until it is hot, then add the oil. Gently pan-fry the fish on each side until it is lightly browned and remove with a spatula. To the remaining oil add the garlic, ginger, rice wine, soy sauce and sesame oil. Return the fish to the wok and gently re-heat. Serve at once.

RICE WINE STEEPED FISH

*F*ish and rice wine go together like love and marriage – perhaps better, because they *always* 'marry' well. The distinct rich wine flavour enhances the fish taste without drowning it; it works much like butter and lemon in certain Western recipes. Once the alcohol has evaporated in the steeping process, there remains the subtle residual rice wine aroma. After the preparation of the sauce, the dish is rapidly completed, producing a simple but elegant meal that is tasty and wholesome. It may be served at a party or at an informal meal for family and friends. The dish re-heats well provided that this is done gently.

SHOPPING LIST
  1 lb (450 g) fresh fish fillets
    (preferably cod or haddock)
  Spring onions

PREPARATION TIME *8 minutes*

COOKING TIME *12 minutes plus 5 minutes' standing time*

SERVES 4

15 fl oz (400 ml) Chinese rice wine or dry sherry
5 fl oz (150 ml) water
2 tablespoons light soy sauce
1 teaspoon freshly ground white pepper
2 teaspoons salt
2 teaspoons sugar
2 teaspoons cornflour mixed with 2 teaspoons cold water
1 lb (450 g) fresh fish fillets
2 teaspoons sesame oil
3 tablespoons finely chopped spring onions

Bring the rice wine, water, soy sauce, pepper, 1 teaspoon of the salt and sugar to the boil in a frying-pan. Reduce the liquid over a high heat to about half its original volume, add the cornflour mixture and cook for 30 seconds.

While the sauce is reducing, rub the fish fillets with the remaining 1 teaspoon of salt and sesame oil and set aside.

Add the fish fillets to the liquid, cover and simmer gently for 2 minutes. Remove the pan from the heat and leave to stand for 5 minutes.

Transfer the fish fillets to a serving platter, pour the sauce over them and sprinkle with the spring onions.

STIR-FRIED PRAWNS AND PEAS

*F*resh uncooked prawns are made for quick cooking. They need little preparation and cooking, and in fact overcooking can ruin their succulence and unique sea flavour. Here they are combined with one of my favourite vegetables, peas, which add colour and a contrasting texture and taste to the dish. Try, as always, to obtain fresh peas; if they are not available, frozen peas work very well. For variety you could use fresh broad beans or fresh sweetcorn kernels instead of peas. This makes a superb luncheon dish accompanied by rice, or it may serve as an elegant starter for a dinner party.

SHOPPING LIST
> *1 lb (450 g) fresh uncooked prawns*
> *8 oz (225 g) fresh peas (shelled weight) or frozen peas*
> *Garlic*
> *Fresh root ginger*
> *Spring onions*

PREPARATION TIME *15 minutes*

COOKING TIME *4–5 minutes*

SERVES *2–4*

1 lb (450 g) fresh uncooked prawns
8 oz (225 g) fresh peas (shelled weight) or frozen peas
1½ tablespoons oil (preferably groundnut)
1 tablespoon coarsely chopped garlic
1 tablespoon coarsely chopped fresh root ginger
2 tablespoons coarsely chopped spring onions
2 teaspoons sesame oil
2 tablespoons water

For the marinade
1 teaspoon salt
1 teaspoon sesame oil

Peel the prawns and discard the shells. Using a small sharp knife, partially split the prawns lengthways and remove the fine digestive cord. Pat the prawns dry with kitchen paper. Mix the marinade ingredients, combine with the prawns and set aside.

If you are using fresh peas, blanch them in boiling water for 2 minutes, drain and set aside. If you are using frozen peas, let them thaw at room temperature.

Heat a wok or large frying-pan, then add the oil. Add garlic, ginger and prawns and stir-fry for 30 seconds. Then add the peas and continue to stir-fry for 1 minute. Finally add spring onions and sesame oil. Add 2 tablespoons of water and stir-fry for another 2 minutes. Serve at once.

FAST CURRIED FISH STEW

*T*his recipe derives from Southeast Asian cuisine, as the zesty seasonings, curry paste and coconut milk used to make it clearly suggest. A stew usually implies long slow cooking, the opposite of quick and easy. In the case of a fish stew, however, this need not be so, especially when such dramatic seasonings are used; the delicate flesh of the fish rapidly absorbs the flavourings, and long simmering is unnecessary. The sauce in this case not only spices up the fish but also keeps it moist and succulent. The result is a quick stew that is warm, savoury and satisfying to the soul as well as pleasing to the palate, just as if it had simmered for hours. The recipe can readily be increased to serve a larger group. In any event, it can rapidly be put together as a main-course dish or as a starter for a special dinner. It can be made a few hours in advance of the meal, if you wish, and re-heated. You may like to add extra vegetables such as courgettes, potatoes or other root vegetables when they are in season.

SHOPPING LIST

*1½ lb (700 g) fresh fish fillets
(preferably cod or haddock)*
8 oz (225 g) carrots
*4 oz (110 g) fresh peas (shelled
weight) or frozen peas*

PREPARATION TIME *15 minutes*

COOKING TIME *12 minutes plus 5
minutes' standing time*

SERVES 4–6

1½ lb (700 g) fresh fish fillets
2½ teaspoons salt
1 teaspoon freshly ground white
or black pepper
2 teaspoons sesame oil
8 oz (225 g) carrots
4 oz (110 g) fresh peas (shelled
weight) or frozen peas
1 × 15 fl oz (400 ml) tin
coconut milk
2 tablespoons curry paste or
powder
2 teaspoons sugar

Cut the fish fillets into 2 inch (5 cm) square chunks, combine them with 2 teaspoons of the salt, the pepper and sesame oil and set aside.

Peel the carrots and cut them into ½ inch (1 cm) cubes. If you are using fresh peas, blanch them in boiling water for 2 minutes, drain and set aside. If you are using frozen peas, let them thaw at room temperature.

Combine the coconut milk, curry paste or powder, remaining ½ teaspoon salt and sugar in a large pan. Bring it to a simmer, add the carrots, cover and cook for 5 minutes or until the carrots are tender. Add the peas and cook for another 1 minute. Finally add the fish chunks, bring the stew to the boil and simmer the mixture for a further 5 minutes. Turn off the heat and let the stew stand, covered, for 5 minutes before serving over plain rice.

10-MINUTE SALMON WITH SPRING ONION SAUCE

Splendid salmon: a favourite with everyone, its noble character lends itself to countless recipes and sauces, but I enjoy it most prepared in a simple and almost unadorned fashion, as in this recipe. The Chinese style is to consume fish neither raw nor overcooked. The aim is to capture the natural flavour, moistness and texture of the fish. The technique of steeping manages this admirably.

This is truly a quick and elegant dish. Serve it as part of a main course for the family (accompanied by an easy vegetable dish and rice) when salmon is in season, or as a starter or main course for a special dinner party. Sea bass or plaice fillets may be substituted for the salmon if you wish.

Shopping List
  1 lb (450 g) fresh salmon fillets
  Spring onions
  Fresh root ginger

Preparation Time *12 minutes*

Cooking Time *6–7 minutes plus 8
  minutes' standing time*

Serves 4

1 lb (450 g) fresh salmon fillets
2 teaspoons salt
½ teaspoon freshly ground
  white or black pepper
1 pint (570 ml) water

For the sauce
6 tablespoons coarsely chopped
  spring onions
1 tablespoon finely chopped
  fresh root ginger
1½ tablespoons oil (preferably
  groundnut)
2 teaspoons sesame oil

Rub the salmon fillets with 1 teaspoon of the salt and the pepper.

Bring the water to a simmer in a frying-pan. Add the salmon, simmer for 2–3 minutes, cover tightly and turn off the heat. Allow to stand for 8 minutes.

Combine the spring onions, ginger and the remaining 1 teaspoon salt together in a small bowl. In a small pan combine the oil and sesame oil and bring it to the smoking point.

Remove salmon from the water and arrange on a platter. Scatter the spring onion mixture on top and pour hot oil over it. Serve at once.

MUSSELS IN BLACK BEAN SAUCE

*M*ussels are an ideal 'quick and easy' food. Once they have been scrubbed clean in cold water to remove all sand, they cook very rapidly, announcing that they are done by cordially opening their shells. Make sure that they are all firmly closed before cooking: throw away any that do not close up when touched or that have damaged shells.

A greater quantity of this dish can easily be prepared for larger gatherings. I prefer to use smaller mussels; if you have a choice, try them.

SHOPPING LIST
  Garlic
  Fresh root ginger
  3 lb (1.4 kg) fresh mussels
  Spring onions

PREPARATION TIME *20 minutes*

COOKING TIME *8–12 minutes*

SERVES 4–6

2 tablespoons oil (preferably groundnut)
4 tablespoons coarsely chopped black beans
3 tablespoons coarsely chopped garlic
2 tablespoons coarsely chopped fresh root ginger
3 lb (1.4 kg) fresh mussels, well scrubbed
2 tablespoons coarsely chopped spring onions
2 teaspoons light soy sauce

Heat a wok or large frying-pan, then add the oil, black beans, garlic and ginger. Stir-fry for 20 seconds and add the mussels. Continue to cook for 5 minutes or until all the mussels have opened. Discard any which have difficulty opening or do not open at all. Add the spring onions and soy sauce. Give the mixture a final stir and serve at once.

STEAMED SALMON WITH BLACK BEAN SAUCE

*F*resh salmon is a luxury but every serious diner deserves it once in a while. Buy it in season when it is least expensive. Prepare it using this Chinese steaming method: it preserves all the noble characteristics of the salmon. Here I serve it with a traditional black bean sauce. It has a very pleasantly pungent taste that actually enhances the distinctive salmon flavour, making a wonderful contrast on the palate. Haddock or cod fillets make a successful substitute for salmon, or you could even try scallops. This simple dish would grace a dinner party as a main course or as a brilliant starter.

SHOPPING LIST
1 lb (450 g) fresh salmon fillets,
1 inch (2.5 cm) thick
Garlic
Fresh root ginger
Spring onions

PREPARATION TIME *10 minutes*

COOKING TIME *10 minutes*

SERVES 4–6

1 lb (450 g) fresh salmon fillets,
   1 inch (2.5 cm) thick
1 teaspoon salt
2 teaspoons sesame oil
1 tablespoon oil (preferably
   groundnut)
2 tablespoons coarsely chopped
   black beans
1½ tablespoons coarsely
   chopped garlic
1 tablespoon finely chopped
   fresh root ginger
3 tablespoons coarsely chopped
   spring onions
1 tablespoon dark soy sauce
2 teaspoons light soy sauce
5 fl oz (150 ml) water
1 teaspoon cornflour mixed
   with 1 teaspoon water

Set a rack into a wok or deep pan. Put in water to a depth of 2½ inches (6 cm) and bring it to a simmer.

Rub the salmon fillets with the salt and sesame oil and place on a heatproof plate that will fit into the wok or pan. Place the plate holding the fish on the rack, cover tightly and steam for about 6 minutes. It is best to undercook the salmon slightly as it continues to cook even after it has been removed from the steamer.

While the salmon is steaming, heat a wok or large frying-pan, then add the oil, black beans, garlic and ginger. Stir-fry the mixture for 1 minute, then add the spring onions, soy sauces and water and simmer for 1 minute. Add the cornflour mixture and stir the sauce until it thickens.

When the salmon is cooked, pour the hot sauce over it and serve at once.

STIR-FRIED SCALLOPS WITH LEEKS

*T*he leek is a member of the onion family and that means it has been used for millennia in China to flavour and enhance other foods. This scallop and leek recipe is a Shanghai-style dish popular in eastern China. Like most shellfish recipes it is simple and easy to make. The leeks need a little more cooking time than the scallops but the combination is quite tasty. For a change, try replacing the scallops with prawns. This is a home-style meal that makes family dining something quite special.

SHOPPING LIST
> *1 lb (450 g) fresh scallops*
> *1 lb (450 g) leeks*
> *Spring onions*
> *Garlic*
> *Fresh root ginger*

PREPARATION TIME *18 minutes*

COOKING TIME *8 minutes*

SERVES 4–6

> 1 lb (450 g) fresh scallops
> 1 lb (450 g) leeks
> 1½ tablespoons oil

2 tablespoons coarsely chopped
   spring onions
1 tablespoon coarsely chopped
   garlic
2 teaspoons finely chopped
   fresh root ginger
½ teaspoon salt

For the sauce
2 tablespoons dark soy sauce
2 teaspoons chilli bean sauce
1 tablespoon Chinese rice wine
   or dry sherry
1 teaspoon sugar
2 teaspoons sesame oil

If the scallops are very large, cut them in half. Dry them with kitchen paper and set aside. Trim the leeks and discard any blemished parts. Cut them into 2 parts at the point where they begin to turn green and discard the green part. Split the white part in half and cut it at a slight diagonal into 2 inch (5 cm) segments. Wash well several times in cold water.

Heat a wok or large frying-pan, then add the oil (preferably groundnut), leeks, spring onions, garlic, ginger and salt and stir-fry for 1 minute. Add the sauce ingredients and stir-fry the mixture for 3 minutes. Lastly, add the scallops and stir-fry for 4 more minutes or until the scallops are just cooked. (They should be slightly firm to the touch; I find them at their best when they are barely cooked through.) Serve at once.

STIR-FRIED PEPPERS WITH SCALLOPS

Scallops are fragile, sweetly delicate morsels and need very little preparation or cooking time. They embody all the qualities aimed for in this book, being quick, easy and delicious. In this recipe I combine them with nutritious, tasty and colourful red and green peppers. The result is a festive-looking dish that belies its ease of preparation: perfect for a family meal or as the centrepiece of a dinner party prepared at short notice.

Mussels or clams may be substituted for the scallops and asparagus, courgettes or mange-tout for the peppers. If you like spicy food, add 2 finely sliced fresh chillies.

SHOPPING LIST
1 lb (450 g) fresh scallops
8 oz (225 g) red peppers
4 oz (110 g) green pepper
Spring onions
Garlic
Fresh root ginger

PREPARATION TIME *15 minutes*

COOKING TIME *8 minutes*

SERVES 4–6

1 lb (450 g) fresh scallops
8 oz (225 g) red peppers
4 oz (110 g) green pepper

1½ tablespoons oil (preferably groundnut)
1½ tablespoons coarsely chopped spring onions
1 tablespoon coarsely chopped garlic
2 teaspoons finely chopped fresh root ginger

For the sauce
1 tablespoon light soy sauce
2 teaspoons yellow bean sauce
2 tablespoons Chinese rice wine or dry sherry
1 teaspoon sugar
1 teaspoon sesame oil

Wash the scallops, pat them dry with kitchen paper and set them aside. De-seed the peppers and cut them into 1 inch (2.5 cm) squares.

Heat a wok or large frying-pan and add the oil, spring onions, garlic and ginger, and stir-fry for 10 seconds. Then add the peppers and stir-fry for 2 minutes. Stir in the scallops and the sauce ingredients. Continue to cook for another 4 minutes. Serve at once.

FRIED FISH WITH WHOLE GARLIC

*L*overs of the 'stinking rose' – and who is not? – understand that whole garlic cloves are among the most delicious and sweetly pungent foods in the world. Garlic adds great dimension to so many different dishes, and to fish in particular. In Shanghai a dish featuring eels and whole garlic is very popular. I have adapted the recipe to use commonly available fish fillets; these work as well and are easy to prepare. If you prefer you can also substitute whole shallots or small onions for the garlic. Serve this dish with rice and stir-fried vegetables for a healthy and very tasty meal.

SHOPPING LIST
  1 lb (450 g) fresh fish fillets
    (preferably cod or haddock)
  Garlic
  Fresh root ginger

PREPARATION TIME *15 minutes*

COOKING TIME *10 minutes*

SERVES 4

  1 lb (450 g) fresh fish fillets
  1 teaspoon salt
  3 tablespoons cornflour

4 tablespoons oil (preferably
    groundnut)
8 cloves garlic, peeled
2 tablespoons coarsely chopped
    fresh root ginger

For the sauce
1 tablespoon Chinese rice wine
    or dry sherry
3 tablespoons water
1 tablespoon light soy sauce
1 tablespoon bean sauce
1 teaspoon sugar
1 tablespoon dark soy sauce

Rub the fish fillets with the salt and cornflour.

Heat a wok or large frying-pan, then add the oil. Fry the fish on both sides until it is golden-brown. Remove the fish and drain on kitchen paper.

Drain all but 1 tablespoon of oil from the pan, add the garlic and ginger and stir-fry for 20 seconds. Then add the sauce ingredients and cook for 3 minutes or until the garlic is tender. Return the fish to the wok and re-heat it. Serve at once with the garlic cloves.

5-MINUTE FISH COOKED ON A PLATE

*T*his highly unusual recipe produces perfectly cooked fish in almost no time at all. The fish is pounded until it is thin (very easy to do) and then actually cooked on the plates which, I hasten to add, must be able to withstand heating to a high temperature! The flattened fish fillets are laid on heated, oiled plates, the heated sauce is added and the fish cooks through in about 5 minutes. Timing and 'touch' are important here; practise this dish a few times before you make it the feature of a dinner party.

SHOPPING LIST
> *1 lb (450 g) fresh fish fillets*
> > *(preferably salmon or tuna)*
>
> *Fresh root ginger*
> *Spring onions*

PREPARATION TIME *15 minutes*

COOKING TIME *10 minutes*

SERVES 4

> 1 lb (450 g) fresh fish fillets
> 5 fl oz (150 ml) Chinese rice
> > wine or dry sherry

3 tablespoons water
1 tablespoon dark soy sauce
1 teaspoon light soy sauce
2 teaspoons finely chopped
> fresh root ginger
2 teaspoons sugar
1 teaspoon sesame oil
1 teaspoon cornflour mixed
> with 1 teaspoon water
1 tablespoon oil (preferably
> groundnut)
3 tablespoons finely chopped
> spring onions

Pre-heat the oven to gas mark 3, 325°F (170°C). Place 4 heatproof plates in the oven and let them heat for 15 minutes.

Divide the fish fillets into 4 portions. Place each one between sheets of cling film and pound gently with a wooden mallet or rolling pin until the thickness of the fish is reduced to ⅛ inch (0.3 cm).

Bring the rice wine, water, soy sauces, ginger, sugar and sesame oil to a simmer. Thicken with the cornflour mixture.

Carefully remove the plates from the oven (they should be very hot). Rub each plate with a little groundnut oil. Place a piece of fish on each plate. Pour some sauce over the top of each piece of fish, sprinkle with the green onions, and leave to stand for 5 minutes to cook through and cool slightly before serving.

Prawns in Ginger Sauce

*A*gain, one of my quick and easy favourites, prawns – this time with a zesty ginger sauce to make a spicy and refreshing treat. This delightful and visually attractive dish can be served over rice for a one-dish meal that will satisfy both the stomach and the palate. It can also double as a starter for a dinner party.

Shopping List
1 lb (450 g) fresh uncooked prawns
Fresh root ginger
Fresh coriander

Preparation Time *20 minutes*

Cooking Time *4 minutes*

Serves 4

1 lb (450 g) fresh uncooked prawns
1 teaspoon salt
1 teaspoon cornflour
1 teaspoon sesame oil
1½ tablespoons oil (preferably groundnut)
3 tablespoons finely chopped fresh root ginger

For the sauce
2 tablespoons Chinese rice wine or dry sherry
1 tablespoon light soy sauce
1 tablespoon water
½ teaspoon salt
1 teaspoon sugar
2 tablespoons finely chopped fresh coriander
2 teaspoons sesame oil

Peel the prawns and discard the shells. Using a small sharp knife, partially split the prawns lengthways and remove the fine digestive cord – if you are particularly short of time you can omit this stage. Pat the prawns dry with kitchen paper and combine them with the salt, cornflour and 1 teaspoon sesame oil.

Heat a wok or large frying-pan, then add the oil, prawns and ginger. Stir-fry the mixture for 30 seconds. Then add the sauce ingredients and continue to cook for 2 minutes. Serve at once.

HOT PEPPER PRAWNS

I was introduced to this dish one evening when I dined with Madhur Jaffrey and her husband at the Shun Lee Palace restaurant in New York. She suggested that I try it, predicting that I would appreciate the imaginative interplay of pungent aromas and spicy flavours. How right she was. This is an exciting treat for the tastebuds and very easy to prepare. Serve it with rice. For a one-dish meal double the quantity of sauce and toss sauce and prawns with fresh egg noodles or rice noodles.

SHOPPING LIST
1 lb (450 g) fresh uncooked
    prawns
2 fresh chillies
Garlic
Spring onions

PREPARATION TIME *18 minutes*

COOKING TIME *4 minutes*

SERVES 4

1 lb (450 g) fresh uncooked
    prawns
1 teaspoon salt
2 teaspoons cornflour

2 teaspoons sesame oil
2 tablespoons oil (preferably
    groundnut)
2 fresh chillies, de-seeded and
    coarsely chopped
1 tablespoon black beans
2 tablespoons coarsely chopped
    garlic
4 tablespoons coarsely chopped
    spring onions
3 tablespoons white rice vinegar
2 tablespoons dark soy sauce
1 tablespoon sugar
2 teaspoons cornflour mixed
    with 2 teaspoons water

Peel the prawns and discard the shells. Using a small sharp knife, partially split the prawns lengthways and remove the fine digestive cord – if time is short, omit this stage. Pat the prawns dry with kitchen paper and combine with the salt, cornflour and sesame oil and mix well.

Heat a wok or large frying-pan and add the oil and prawns. Stir-fry for 1 minute, then remove the prawns with a slotted spoon. To the remaining oil add the chillies, black beans, garlic and spring onions. Stir-fry for 20 seconds and add the vinegar, soy sauce and sugar. Stir in the cornflour mixture and return the prawns to the wok. Cook for another 2 minutes and serve at once.

WHOLE PRAWNS BAKED IN SALT

*T*his does *not* produce a 'salty' dish. Rather, the salt, being very hot, cooks the unpeeled prawns quickly with just the right amount of savour. The result is very fresh-tasting prawns, with a special aroma ready for the contrasting flavours of the dipping sauce. Serve the cooked prawns immediately so that they do not absorb too much salt, and let your guests peel their own. This quick and easy dish is perfect for a large crowd.

SHOPPING LIST

1 lb (450 g) fresh uncooked
prawns
1 lb (450 g) coarse sea salt
Fresh root ginger

PREPARATION TIME *10 minutes*

COOKING TIME *10 minutes*

SERVES 4

1 lb (450 g) fresh uncooked
prawns
1 lb (450 g) coarse sea salt

For the dipping sauce
3 tablespoons finely chopped
fresh root ginger
5 tablespoons black rice vinegar

Rinse the prawns thoroughly under cold running water. Do not peel. Pat the prawns dry with kitchen paper. Combine the dipping sauce ingredients and set aside.

Heat a wok or large frying-pan, then add the sea salt. Heat the salt until it is very hot and popping, add the prawns and stir, mixing them thoroughly with the salt. When the prawns are pink and firm, they are cooked. This should take about 5–8 minutes. Immediately remove the prawns from the pan, shaking off any excess salt. Serve at once with the dipping sauce.

4

POULTRY

*C*hicken, duck, pigeon, pheasant and quail: poultry in its many forms has been central to the Chinese cuisine for millennia. And the Chinese, in my opinion, are the world's experts in cooking poultry. All parts of each bird are used and, after cooking has transformed them, prized: the wings, the entrails, even the feet!

In the West we do not have such a wide variety of poultry so easily available and many of the game birds require extensive preparation not appropriate to the 'quick and easy' approach. Thus here I stay with what I have elsewhere called 'the sweet bird of our youth' – chicken. Of all poultry it is the most accessible and adaptable. It is relatively inexpensive, easy to cook and goes well with almost every other food. With its own delicate taste and great receptivity to other flavours, it lends itself to many recipes. Here I use parts of the chicken that are easy to cook, such as breasts and wings. Where longer cooking is required or expedient, I use chicken thighs. I have also included a few turkey recipes here – turkey is another nutritious and versatile food and deserves a bigger place in our diet.

RED-COOKED CHICKEN WINGS

'Red-cooking' simply means simmering in a richly flavoured sauce that also imparts a deep red colour to the food. Here I use chicken wings, the tastiest and most under-rated part of the bird – and the result is a tempting dish, nicely re-heatable and quick to make, taking only about 30 minutes. You can use chicken thighs and drumsticks instead of wings if you wish, but they will need a slightly longer cooking time.

SHOPPING LIST
> *1½ lb (700 g) chicken wings*
> *Fresh root ginger*
> *Garlic*

PREPARATION TIME *14 minutes*

COOKING TIME *15 minutes*

SERVES 4–6

1½ lb (700 g) chicken wings
1 tablespoon oil (preferably groundnut)
1 tablespoon coarsely chopped fresh root ginger
1 tablespoon coarsely chopped garlic
½ teaspoon salt
2 tablespoons dark soy sauce
1 tablespoon Chinese rice wine or dry sherry
3 tablespoons hoisin sauce
2 teaspoons sugar
2 teaspoons chilli bean sauce
5 fl oz (150 ml) water

Cut the chicken wings in half at the joint.

Heat a wok or large frying-pan, then add the oil, ginger, garlic, and salt. Stir-fry the mixture for 10 seconds. Add all the other ingredients except the wings and simmer for 1 minute. Put in the wings, cover the wok and cook for 15 minutes or until the wings are cooked through. Serve at once or allow to cool and serve at room temperature.

STIR-FRIED CHICKEN LIVERS WITH ONIONS

*C*hicken livers are among the easiest foods to prepare. The trick is to combine them with the proper seasonings and spices so that their delicateness is retained but they are also given a new dimension. Hence the onions and the five-spice powder in this recipe – and it works! Serve this dish as part of a Chinese meal or as a main course with rice and a vegetable. Calf's liver may be substituted for the chicken livers if you wish.

SHOPPING LIST
> *1 lb (450 g) chicken livers*
> *2 onions*

PREPARATION TIME *14 minutes*

COOKING TIME *11 minutes*

SERVES 2–4

1 lb (450 g) chicken livers
1 tablespoon plus 2 teaspoons Chinese rice wine or dry sherry
1 tablespoon light soy sauce
½ teaspoon five-spice powder
1 teaspoon salt
¼ teaspoon freshly ground black pepper
1 tablespoon cornflour
2 teaspoons plus 1 tablespoon oil (preferably groundnut)
2 onions, peeled and sliced
2 teaspoons sesame oil

Cut the chicken livers into bite-sized pieces. Combine the livers with 1 tablespoon of the rice wine, the soy sauce, five-spice powder, ½ teaspoon of the salt, the pepper and cornflour. Mix well.

Heat a wok or large frying-pan, then add 2 teaspoons of the oil. Stir-fry the livers for about 4 minutes or until they are brown on the outside but still pink inside. Remove the livers from the wok. Wipe the wok clean, then re-heat. Add the remaining 1 tablespoon oil, ½ teaspoon salt and the onions. Stir-fry for 4 minutes or until the onions are brown and slightly caramelised. Return the livers to the wok and add the remaining 2 teaspoons rice wine and the sesame oil. Stir-fry for 2 more minutes. Serve at once.

QUICK CHINESE CHICKEN SALAD

*M*ost of the work for this dish can be done well in advance, so that when it is time to eat you have a true quick and easy treat. Once the sauce is made and the chicken cooked, you are a few minutes from enjoying a delightful chicken salad. It is ideal for entertaining or for a light luncheon.

SHOPPING LIST
  12 oz (350 g) chicken breasts
  8 oz (225 g) Iceberg lettuce
  Garlic
  Fresh root ginger
  Spring onions

PREPARATION TIME *25 minutes*

COOKING TIME *8 minutes plus 10 minutes' standing time*

SERVES 2–4

12 oz (350 g) chicken breasts
2 teaspoons salt
8 oz (225 g) Iceberg lettuce, finely shredded
2 tablespoons rice wine vinegar

For the sauce
1 clove garlic, peeled
1 slice fresh root ginger, peeled
2 spring onions, green tops removed
2 teaspoons chilli bean sauce
2 teaspoons dark soy sauce
1 teaspoon sugar
2 teaspoons white rice vinegar
2 teaspoons sesame paste or peanut butter
½ teaspoon salt
½ teaspoon freshly ground black pepper
2 teaspoons sesame oil

Remove the skin from the chicken breasts and place them in a pan. Put in enough cold water to cover the chicken and add the salt. Bring the mixture to a simmer and cook for 5 minutes. Turn off the heat and cover tightly. Leave the chicken to stand in the hot water for 10 minutes.

Meanwhile, put all the sauce ingredients into a blender and blend well. Set aside. Toss the lettuce with the rice wine vinegar and place on a serving platter.

Remove the chicken from its cooking liquid and allow to cool.

Pull the meat off the bone, shred it finely and toss it with the sauce. Place the chicken and the sauce on top of the lettuce and serve at once.

STIR-FRIED SMOKED CHICKEN WITH CHINESE LEAVES

*S*moked chicken and duck are very popular in China. Such delicacies require a time-consuming process of smoking that, fortunately, is done for us. Smoked chicken and duck are readily available in supermarkets and speciality food shops. Thus we can turn a complex recipe into something quick and easy as in this dish, a north Chinese favourite, easy to make and very pleasing to the eye and the palate. Courgettes, mange-tout, peppers or carrots may be used instead of Chinese leaves. With rice and a salad the dish makes a substantial and nutritious meal.

SHOPPING LIST
1½ lb (700 g) smoked chicken
1 lb (450 g) Chinese leaves
Garlic
Fresh root ginger

PREPARATION TIME *15 minutes*

COOKING TIME *8 minutes*

SERVES 4–6

1½ lb (700 g) smoked chicken
1 lb (450 g) Chinese leaves
1½ tablespoons oil (preferably groundnut)
3 tablespoons coarsely chopped garlic
1 tablespoon coarsely chopped fresh root ginger
1 tablespoon dark soy sauce
1 tablespoon Chinese rice wine or dry sherry

With your fingers tear the meat from the bones of the chicken. Cut it into large shreds and set aside. Discard the bones. Coarsely chop the Chinese leaves.

Heat a wok or large frying-pan, then add the oil, garlic and ginger. Stir-fry the mixture for 10 seconds and add the Chinese leaves. Continue to stir-fry for 5 minutes, add the soy sauce and rice wine and cook for another minute. Then add the smoked chicken and cook through. Serve at once.

CHINESE BARBECUED CHICKEN

*W*hen warm weather calls you out of doors, it is appropriate to enjoy cooking and eating outside – summer is the time for barbecueing and this recipe calls for the barbecue, though you can, of course, cook it indoors under your kitchen grill. Chinese seasonings and spices add new dimensions to any barbecued food, and with this recipe most of the work can be done well in advance. The cooking time is a short 25 minutes, during which you can prepare a salad or stir-fried vegetable dish and perhaps some rice to accompany the chicken. The quantities given below can easily be doubled to feed a larger crowd and the chicken makes wonderfully exotic picnic fare if served cold.

SHOPPING LIST
1 × 3–3½ lb (1.4–1.6 kg)
   chicken
Garlic
Fresh root ginger

PREPARATION TIME *10 minutes. 1 hour marinating time*

COOKING TIME *25 minutes*

SERVES 4

1 × 3–3½ lb (1.4–1.6 kg) chicken
2 teaspoons salt
4 cloves garlic, peeled
2 slices fresh root ginger
5 tablespoons hoisin sauce
3 tablespoons Chinese rice wine or dry sherry
1 tablespoon dark soy sauce
1 tablespoon light soy sauce
1 teaspoon chilli bean sauce
2 teaspoons sugar
2 teaspoons sesame oil

Cut the chicken into quarters and rub each piece evenly with the salt. Combine the rest of the ingredients in a blender and purée them. Rub this mixture over the chicken and leave to marinate for at least 1 hour or overnight. To speed up the cooking process, bring the marinated chicken to room temperature before barbecueing or grilling.

Pre-heat the barbecue or grill. When it is hot, cook the chicken leg quarters for 15 minutes, watching carefully to make sure that they do not burn. Then add the breast quarters and continue cooking for 10 minutes. Serve hot or allow to cool and serve at room temperature.

MINCED TURKEY PATTIES

*I*n China, turkey is virtually unknown. I believe that the Chinese palate would find it rather bland and tasteless, lacking the grace and delicateness of chicken. But I think turkey is a versatile food that needs only a little care and imaginative seasonings to make it quite delectable. Turkey breast is also ideal for quick cooking. The preparation of this dish takes a little time, but the spices and seasonings do enliven the turkey and the actual cooking time is quite short. You can, if you wish, make the patties several hours in advance and leave them, covered with cling film, in the refrigerator until you are ready to cook them. The patties make an excellent starter dish.

SHOPPING LIST

   1 lb (450 g) boneless turkey
     breasts
   Garlic
   Fresh root ginger
   Spring onions
   Fresh coriander
   1 egg

PREPARATION TIME *22 minutes*

COOKING TIME *6 minutes*

SERVES 4

1 lb (450 g) boneless turkey
  breasts
1 teaspoon salt
½ teaspoon freshly ground
  white or black pepper
2 tablespoons coarsely chopped
  garlic
1 tablespoon coarsely chopped
  fresh root ginger
4 tablespoons finely chopped
  spring onions
3 tablespoons finely chopped
  fresh coriander
1 tablespoon cornflour
1 egg white
3 tablespoons oil (preferably
  groundnut)

For the sauce
2 tablespoons Chinese rice
  wine or dry sherry
2 tablespoons water
3 tablespoons oyster sauce

Coarsely chop the turkey breasts in a food processor or by hand. If you chop them in a food processor, be sure to use the pulse so that the flesh is not over-processed: it should have the texture of minced beef. Mix in the salt, pepper, garlic, ginger, spring onions, coriander, cornflour and egg white. Form the mixture into small round patties about 3 inches (7.5 cm) in diameter.

Heat a wok or large frying-pan, then add the oil. Fry the patties for about 2 minutes on each side or until they are nicely browned. Drain them on kitchen paper. Pour off the fat from the wok, then pour in the sauce ingredients. Bring to a simmer and return the patties to the wok to warm through in the sauce. Serve at once.

STIR-FRIED TURKEY WITH PEPPERS

*H*ere again I substitute nutritious, low-fat turkey meat for chicken and it works wonderfully as a stir-fried meal. The red peppers add spice and colour to this wholesome and inexpensive dish, though you can success-fully substitute green peppers or even courgettes if these are not available.

SHOPPING LIST
  1 lb (450 g) turkey breast
  1 lb (450 g) red peppers

PREPARATION TIME *10 minutes*

COOKING TIME *4–5 minutes*

SERVES 2–4

1 lb (450 g) turkey breast
1 lb (450 g) red peppers
1½ tablespoons oil (preferably groundnut)
2 tablespoons Chinese rice wine or dry sherry
½ teaspoon salt
1 tablespoon oyster sauce

For the marinade
1½ tablespoons light soy sauce
1 tablespoon Chinese rice wine or dry sherry
2 teaspoons sesame oil
2 teaspoons cornflour

Cut the turkey breast into ½ × 3 inch (1 × 7.5 cm) cubes. Combine with the marinade ingredients in a medium-sized bowl and leave to stand for 5 minutes. De-seed the red peppers and cut them into ½ inch (1 cm) wide strips. Set aside.

Heat a wok or large frying-pan, then add the oil. Add the turkey and stir-fry for 10 seconds. Then add the pepper strips and stir-fry for another 10 seconds. Finally add the rice wine, salt, and oyster sauce and continue to stir-fry for 2–3 minutes. Remember that the turkey will continue to cook for a short time after it is removed from the wok so under-cook rather than over-cook it and risk it becoming dry. Serve at once.

CRISPY CHICKEN IN GARLIC-GINGER SAUCE

*H*ere is a dish that is quick and easy and still combines most of the qualities which make Chinese food so appealing: contrasting tastes and textures; dipping sauces; crisp outside, tender inside; lightness and the ability to satisfy at the same time. Most of the work is in the preparation, with just a few minutes' cooking time – in fact you can prepare the chicken and sauce several hours before you are ready to cook. Serve this as a main course with rice and a simple salad.

SHOPPING LIST
1½ lb (700 g) chicken thighs
Spring onions
Garlic
Fresh root ginger

PREPARATION TIME *20 minutes*

COOKING TIME *7 minutes*

SERVES 4–6

1½ lb (700 g) chicken thighs
2 tablespoons light soy sauce
2 tablespoons Chinese rice
  wine or dry sherry
3 tablespoons coarsely chopped
  spring onions
2 tablespoons coarsely chopped
  garlic
1 tablespoon coarsely chopped
  fresh root ginger
15 fl oz (400 ml) oil
Cornflour for dusting

For the sauce
1 tablespoon light soy sauce
1 tablespoon sugar
1 tablespoon white rice vinegar
2 teaspoons sesame oil

Bone the chicken thighs by running a knife through to the bone along their length, then opening each side of the meat, exposing the bone. Combine the chicken with the soy sauce and rice wine.

Combine the spring onions, garlic and ginger in one bowl and combine the sauce ingredients in another.

Heat a wok or large frying-pan, then add the oil (preferably groundnut). Dust the chicken pieces with the cornflour and deep-fry for 5 minutes or until golden-brown. Remove from the wok and drain on kitchen paper, then place on a serving platter and keep warm. Drain all the oil from the wok and re-heat it. Add the spring onions, garlic and ginger and stir-fry for 20 seconds. Pour in the sauce ingredients and cook for a further 20 seconds. Serve the chicken with the sauce on the side.

Quick Pan-fried Five-spice Fish (page 42)
Stir-fried Peppers with Scallops (page 51)
Steamed Salmon with Black Bean Sauce (page 48)

Overleaf, clockwise from top:
Savoury Custard with Pork, Spring Onions and Oyster Sauce (page 91)
Stir-fried Beef with Onions and Mint (page 87)
Chinese Lamb Curry (page 82)
Stir-fried Smoked Chicken with Chinese Leaves (page 61)
Chicken Thigh Casserole with Orange (page 74)
Minced Turkey Patties (page 63)

STERLING DOUGHTY'S
STIR-FRIED KIWI CHICKEN

Sterling Doughty, of Geneva, Switzerland, is an avid admirer of Chinese cookery. He shares his thoughts on cooking and his recipes – including this one – with me. I immediately saw that it fits into the 'quick and easy' category. The kiwi fruit, becoming less and less exotic to us, needs very little cooking and blends nicely with the delicate chicken breast flavour. Try substituting mango or papaya for the kiwi fruit sometimes – they make a nice alternative.

SHOPPING LIST
>   *1 lb (450 g) boneless chicken*
>   *breasts*
>   *Garlic*
>   *2 kiwi fruit*

PREPARATION TIME *10 minutes*

COOKING TIME *4 minutes*

SERVES 4–6

1 lb (450 g) boneless chicken
    breasts
1 teaspoon salt
1 teaspoon cornflour
1 tablespoon oil (preferably
    groundnut)
2 tablespoons coarsely chopped
    garlic
1 teaspoon chilli bean sauce
1 teaspoon sugar
2 kiwi fruit, peeled and
    quartered
1 teaspoon sesame oil

Red-cooked Winter Vegetables (page 99)
Potatoes in Curry-coconut stew (page 111)
Fast Mange-tout with Mushrooms (page 108)

Cut the chicken into ½ inch (1 cm) cubes. Combine the chicken with the salt and cornflour. Prepare the other ingredients.

Heat a wok or large frying-pan, then add the oil and garlic. Stir-fry for 10 seconds and add the chicken. Stir-fry for 2 minutes, then add the chilli bean sauce, sugar and kiwi fruit. Stir and mix for 1 minute. Finally, add the sesame oil and give the mixture one good stir. Serve at once.

BRAISED CHICKEN AND MUSHROOM CASSEROLE

*Y*es, clearly this takes a little longer than the average quick and easy meal but it is one of my mother's favourites and it *is* delicious. I recall my mother making it on winter mornings before she left for work, placing it with rice on the heater to keep warm so I could eat it for lunch. It is a savoury dish that re-heats well and is worth the extra time and effort. The chicken thighs are robust enough to take the longer cooking and the seasonings.

SHOPPING LIST

    1½ lb (700 g) chicken thighs
    8 oz (225 g) onions
    Garlic
    Fresh root ginger

PREPARATION TIME *23 minutes*

COOKING TIME *11 minutes*

SERVES 4–6

1 oz (25 g) Chinese dried
  mushrooms
1½ pints (900 ml) warm water
1½ lb (700 g) chicken thighs
1 tablespoon oil (preferably
  groundnut)
8 oz (225 g) onions, peeled and
  sliced
2 tablespoons coarsely chopped
  garlic
1 tablespoon coarsely chopped
  fresh root ginger
2 tablespoons Chinese rice
  wine or dry sherry
4 tablespoons oyster sauce

Soak the dried mushrooms in the warm water for 20 minutes until soft. While the mushrooms are soaking, remove the skin and bones from the chicken thighs and discard. Cut the flesh into 1 inch (2.5 cm) cubes. Prepare the rest of the ingredients.

Squeeze the excess liquid from the mushrooms and remove and discard the stalks. Cut the caps into quarters. Save the soaking liquid.

Heat a wok or large frying-pan, then add the oil and chicken. Stir-fry for 3½ minutes or until the chicken begins to brown. Pour off any excess fat, re-heat the wok, add the onions, garlic, ginger and mushrooms and stir-fry for 2 minutes. Then add 5 fl oz (150 ml) of the liquid in which the mushrooms were soaked, the rice wine and oyster sauce. Continue cooking over high heat for 5 minutes. Serve at once.

CURRIED BAKED CHICKEN THIGHS

Curry is a popular seasoning in south China; baking, however, is a rarely used technique – ovens are found only in commercial bakeries. This is a pity for the Chinese because baking is a very convenient method of cooking: place everything in the dish and into the oven and off you go to do other things while the meal looks after itself. In China this would be a clay-pot meal. Here I have combined simple but dramatic flavours to create an unusual curry dish. With rice and a vegetable or salad, it makes a complete and sustaining meal which takes less than 1 hour to prepare. To make an even more substantial meal, bake 8 oz (225 g) finely diced and blanched potatoes and carrots along with the chicken. You can substitute chicken breasts for the thighs but remember that they will take only about 15 minutes to cook.

SHOPPING LIST
  2 lb (900 g) chicken thighs
  Fresh root ginger

PREPARATION TIME *10 minutes*

COOKING TIME *35 minutes*

SERVES 4

  2 lb (900 g) chicken thighs

For the curry sauce
2 tablespoons Madras curry
  paste
1 tablespoon light soy sauce
1 tablespoon finely chopped
  garlic
1 tablespoon finely chopped
  fresh root ginger
1 tablespoon Chinese rice wine
  or dry sherry
2 teaspoons sugar
1 teaspoon salt
1 teaspoon sesame oil

Pre-heat the oven to gas mark 9, 475°F (240°C).

Remove the skin from the thighs and discard it. Place the thighs in a roasting tin or ovenproof dish. Add all the sauce ingredients and mix thoroughly, making sure that the thighs are completely coated.

Bake the thighs for 15 minutes. Turn them over and continue to cook for another 15–20 minutes, depending on how well done you like your chicken. Serve at once.

CHICKEN THIGH CASSEROLE WITH ORANGE

*T*his is an 'overnighter'. My mother used to make it the night before and simply re-heat it at dinner time. She used dried orange peel but I like the clean taste of fresh oranges. The easiest way to remove the rind thinly is with a vegetable peeler. Then pile the resulting pieces of rind on top of each other and cut into thin strips with a sharp knife.

Prepare the dish the day before you need it, when you have some time, then just re-heat this rich and delicious treat – a perfect meal for a cold winter's eve.

SHOPPING LIST
  2 lb (900 g) chicken thighs
  Garlic
  Fresh root ginger
  2 oranges

PREPARATION TIME *20 minutes*

COOKING TIME *24 minutes*

SERVES 4

2 lb (900 g) chicken thighs
1½ tablespoons oil (preferably groundnut)
1 tablespoon finely chopped garlic
1 tablespoon finely chopped fresh root ginger
2 tablespoons black beans
2 teaspoons orange rind, cut into thin strips
5 fl oz (150 ml) orange juice
2 tablespoons light soy sauce
2 teaspoons chilli bean sauce

Remove the skin from the chicken thighs.

Heat a large, heavy, flameproof casserole, then add the oil. Quickly brown the chicken thighs on both sides. Push the thighs to the side of the casserole, then add the garlic, ginger, black beans and orange rind. Stir for 30 seconds. Add the orange juice, soy sauce and chilli bean sauce. Bring the mixture to the boil, then lower the heat to a simmer. Cover the casserole tightly and continue to cook for about 20 minutes. Serve at once.

SPICY HOT CHICKEN WITH BASIL

*T*his is a savoury, almost lusty chicken dish of Southeast Asian provenance. Chicken thighs, with their darker, firmer meat, lend themselves to marinades and longer cooking. I enjoy their more robust chicken flavour and their more substantial texture. Chicken combines nicely with all spices but I particularly enjoy the surprise here of the anise-flavoured basil which is so nice a counterpoint to the other spices. If basil is unavailable, you can substitute fresh mint. Serve the dish with plain rice and a salad or green vegetable for a complete meal. It can be made in advance and stored in the refrigerator as it re-heats well.

SHOPPING LIST
  *1 lb (450 g) chicken thigh meat
    or 2 lb (900g) unboned
    chicken thighs*
  Garlic
  Fresh basil

PREPARATION TIME *25 minutes*

COOKING TIME *10 minutes*

SERVES 4

1 lb (450 g) chicken thigh meat
  or 2 lb (900 g) unboned
  chicken thighs
2 teaspoons light soy sauce
2 teaspoons cornflour
1 teaspoon sesame oil
1½ tablespoons oil (preferably
  groundnut)
2 tablespoons coarsely chopped
  garlic
2 teaspoons chilli bean sauce
2 teaspoons hoisin sauce
2 teaspoons oyster sauce
1 teaspoon dark soy sauce
1 teaspoon sugar
Large handful fresh basil leaves

Remove the skin and bones from the chicken thighs or ask your butcher to do it for you. Cut the chicken into 1 inch (2.5 cm) chunks and combine it in a bowl with the light soy sauce, cornflour and sesame oil.

Heat a wok or large frying-pan and add the oil. When the oil is hot, add the chicken. Stir-fry for 5 minutes, then remove the chicken and drain off the oil. Return the drained chicken to the wok and add all the remaining ingredients except the basil leaves. Cook for another 5 minutes, stirring from time to time. When the chicken is cooked, add the basil, and stir well. Transfer to a serving platter and serve at once.

QUICK ORANGE-LEMON CHICKEN

Orange and lemon are wonderful flavours that chicken breasts readily absorb and blend with. This is a classic quick and easy meal, quite satisfying as a main course with plain rice and a salad. Alternatively, serve it at room temperature as part of a cold buffet or as exotic picnic fare.

SHOPPING LIST
    12 oz (350 g) boneless chicken
        breasts
    Garlic
    Fresh root ginger
    1 orange
    1 lemon
    Spring onions

PREPARATION TIME *15 minutes*

COOKING TIME *5 minutes*

SERVES 2

12 oz (350 g) boneless chicken
    breasts
Salt
1 tablespoon oil (preferably
    groundnut)
2 tablespoons coarsely chopped
    garlic
1 teaspoon finely chopped fresh
    root ginger
2 teaspoons finely chopped
    orange rind
2 teaspoons finely chopped
    lemon rind
4 tablespoons orange juice
4 tablespoons lemon juice
1 tablespoon light soy sauce
1 tablespoon sugar
1 teaspoon cornflour mixed
    with 1 teaspoon water
1 teaspoon chilli bean sauce
2 teaspoons sesame oil
3 tablespoons coarsely chopped
    spring onions

Remove the skin from the chicken and cut the meat into long strips. Blanch the chicken for 30 seconds in a pan of boiling, salted water. Drain and set aside.

Heat a wok or large frying-pan, then add the oil, garlic and ginger. Stir-fry the mixture for 10 seconds and add the rest of the ingredients except for the chicken. Bring the mixture to a simmer, add the chicken to the wok and cook through. Remember that the chicken will continue to cook for at least 30 seconds after you have removed it from the wok, so be sure not to over-cook it. Serve at once.

5

MEAT

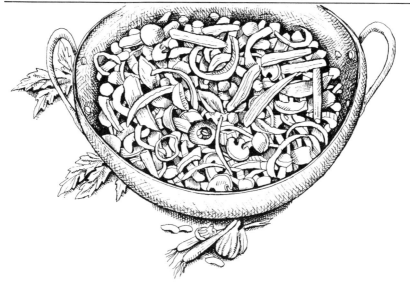

*M*eat is a very popular food in China but it is not consumed in such quantities as in the West. That is, it is rarely the central dish in any meal. Rather, it is used to accompany and to complement other foods – vegetables and rice, for example – or in sauces and soups. This makes for a very healthy diet: in the West we use too much animal protein, at the cost of the vegetable nutrients and food fibre our bodies require.

The Chinese prepare meat in a number of basic ways: steaming, stir-frying, braising and frying are the techniques most often used. Meat is almost always cut into small pieces or thin slices. This makes for minimum cooking and maximum retention of natural flavours and juices. 'Quick and easy' is the general rule in China for the preparation of meat.

The recipes here may readily be offered as main courses. In some cases, which I note, the dishes can be made well ahead of time and re-heated when needed. All of them are delectable and none is too complicated. I indicate which ones go well with rice and thus quite naturally can be part of a one-dish meal, with perhaps a favourite salad.

FAST SPICY MEAT SAUCE FOR NOODLES

Simplicity itself, this marvellously tasty meat sauce transforms a lowly plate of noodles into an impressive meal. If you expect a large crowd, simply expand the recipe proportionately. The sauce freezes well, so you could make several batches and freeze those you do not need immediately. You can substitute minced beef for the pork if you wish. For quick and successful informal entertaining, this dish cannot be beaten.

SHOPPING LIST
Garlic
Spring onions
Fresh root ginger
1 lb (450 g) minced pork

PREPARATION TIME *10–15 minutes*

COOKING TIME *8 minutes*

SERVES 4–6

1½ tablespoons oil
2 tablespoons coarsely chopped garlic
3 tablespoons coarsely chopped spring onions
2 tablespoons coarsely chopped fresh root ginger
1 lb (450 g) minced pork
1 tablespoon chilli bean sauce
1 tablespoon dark soy sauce
2 tablespoons Chinese rice wine or dry sherry
2 tablespoons hoisin sauce
1 teaspoon salt
2 teaspoons sugar

Heat a wok or large frying-pan, then add the oil. Add the garlic, spring onions and ginger and stir-fry for 1 minute. Then add the pork and stir-fry for 2 minutes. Add the chilli bean sauce, soy sauce, rice wine, hoisin sauce, salt and sugar and continue to cook for another 5 minutes. Serve with noodles or over rice.

GRILLED LAMB CHOPS WITH CHINESE MARINADE

Grilling is a popular Western cooking technique, whether outdoors on the barbecue or indoors in the kitchen. Grilled foods cook quickly and easily and, as a bonus, the juices and flavour of meat are sealed inside during grilling by the searing heat. In this recipe the Chinese seasonings permeate the meat, resulting in a very tasty dish – still definitely lamb, but with a spicy twist. Serve it with vegetables or salad and your favourite bread.

For a more quickly grilled meal substitute chicken breasts, which should cut the cooking time down to about 7 minutes.

SHOPPING LIST
1 lb (450 g) thick lamb chops
Garlic
Fresh root ginger
Spring onions

PREPARATION TIME *10 minutes*

COOKING TIME *10-15 minutes*

SERVES 2

1 lb (450 g) thick lamb chops
½ teaspoon salt

For the marinade
1 tablespoon finely chopped garlic
2 teaspoons finely chopped fresh root ginger
3 tablespoons finely chopped spring onions
2 tablespoons Chinese rice wine or dry sherry
1 tablespoon hoisin sauce
1 tablespoon light soy sauce

Pre-heat the grill until it is very hot.

Lightly salt the lamb chops.

Mix the marinade ingredients together in a small bowl. Rub the lamb chops on both sides with the marinade and leave to stand for 5 minutes. Then grill the lamb chops to your taste, turning them half-way through the cooking time. Serve at once.

CHINESE LAMB CURRY

*L*amb is typically a northern Chinese food but the ingenious chefs of the south have taken it and blended it with a familiar Southeast Asian seasoning, curry. This combination appeals to the Southern Chinese palate: curry is a familiar seasoning and assertive enough to mask the strong taste of the lamb, a taste that most Chinese do not particularly relish.

Chinese Lamb Curry is excellent for entertaining because it can be prepared ahead of time and simply re-heated when needed – and it is even tastier then. If you wish, you can prepare the dish in advance up to the point at which the vegetables are added and complete it, cooking the vegetables, just before you are ready to serve. It goes well with rice and perhaps a salad.

SHOPPING LIST

    2½ lb (1.25 kg) breast of lamb
    Garlic
    Fresh root ginger
    1 lb (450 g) potatoes
    8 oz (225 g) carrots

PREPARATION TIME *18 minutes*

COOKING TIME *45 minutes*

SERVES 4–6

2½ lb (1.25 kg) breast of lamb
1½ tablespoons oil (preferably groundnut)
2 tablespoons coarsely chopped garlic
1 tablespoon coarsely chopped fresh root ginger
1 pint (570 ml) water
3 tablespoons light soy sauce
2 tablespoons dark soy sauce
6 tablespoons Madras curry paste or powder
1 tablespoon sugar
1 lb (450 g) potatoes
8 oz (225 g) carrots

Cut the lamb meat from the bone and then cube it. Blanch it in boiling water for 10 minutes. Drain and place in a flameproof casserole.

Heat a wok or large frying-pan, then add the oil, garlic and ginger and stir-fry for 10 seconds. Add the water, soy sauces, curry paste or powder and sugar and bring the mixture to the boil. Pour the liquid over the lamb in the casserole and bring to the boil again. Cover and simmer for 35 minutes or until the meat is tender.

Peel the potatoes and cut them into 1 inch (2.5 cm) cubes. Peel the carrots and cut them into 1 inch (2.5 cm) lengths. Skim the fat from the curry and add the vegetables. Cook for another 10 minutes or until the vegetables are tender, then serve.

TOMATO BEEF WITH ONIONS

I learned to make this quick and easy dish in my uncle's restaurant. I still make it when tomatoes are in season. It is a wonderful combination of two good foods, bound together by the richness of the seasonings and the oyster sauce. Serve it over egg noodles or plain rice.

SHOPPING LIST
>*1 lb (450 g) lean beef steak*
>*8 oz (225 g) onions*
>*1 lb (450 g) tomatoes*

PREPARATION TIME *15 minutes*

COOKING TIME *10 minutes*

SERVES 4–6

1 lb (450 g) lean beef steak
1 tablespoon light soy sauce
2 teaspoons Chinese rice wine
  or dry sherry
2 teaspoons cornflour
8 oz (225 g) onions
1 lb (450 g) tomatoes
2 tablespoons oil (preferably
  groundnut)
2 tablespoons water
3 tablespoons oyster sauce

Cut the beef into thick ¼ × 2 inch (0.5 × 5 cm) slices and put them into a bowl. Add the soy sauce, rice wine and cornflour and mix well.
Peel the onions and cut into thick slices. Quarter the tomatoes.
Heat a wok or large frying-pan, then pour in the oil. Add the beef and stir-fry for 2 minutes to brown. Remove the beef with a slotted spoon and set aside. Add the onions to the wok and stir-fry for 1 minute. Pour in the water and cook for 3 minutes. Drain the juices from the beef into the wok. Continue to cook for another 2 minutes. Add the tomatoes and oyster sauce and cook until the tomatoes are just heated through (they should not be allowed to become mushy). Return the beef to the wok, heat through and serve at once.

BEEF WITH GINGER AND PINEAPPLE

*T*his recipe is derived from the original I enjoyed at Lai Ching Heen, the marvellous Chinese restaurant in Hong Kong's Regent Hotel. I regard it as exemplary of the innovative New Hong Kong Cuisine, in which new ingredients and techniques are being employed to transform traditional recipes. A mouthwatering combination of tastes and textures, it is remarkably easy to prepare and is most appropriate for a dinner party or any special meal. You can, if you wish, prepare the meat, vegetables and fruit in advance and store them, well wrapped, in the refrigerator until you are ready to cook.

SHOPPING LIST
1 lb (450 g) lean beef steak
8 oz (225 g) fresh pineapple
2 red peppers
Spring onions
Fresh root ginger

PREPARATION TIME *21 minutes*

COOKING TIME *8 minutes*

SERVES 4–6

1 lb (450 g) lean beef steak
1 teaspoon salt
4 teaspoons Chinese rice wine
   or dry sherry
4 teaspoons sesame oil
1½ teaspoons cornflour
8 oz (225 g) fresh pineapple
2 red peppers
2 spring onions
2 tablespoons oil (preferably
   groundnut)
2 tablespoons shredded fresh
   root ginger
1 tablespoon water
1 teaspoon light soy sauce

Cut the beef into thick ¼ × 2 inch (0.5 × 5 cm) slices and put them into a bowl. Add the salt, 2 teaspoons of the rice wine, 2 teaspoons of the sesame oil and the cornflour and mix well.

Peel the pineapple and cut it into thick slices, discarding the tough core. De-seed the peppers and cut them into wedges. Cut the spring onions into 3 inch (7.5 cm) lengths.

Heat a wok or large frying-pan, then pour in the oil. Add the beef and stir-fry for 1 minute to brown. Remove the beef with a slotted spoon and set aside. Add the ginger, peppers and spring onions to the wok and stir-fry for 1 minute. Pour in the water, the remaining 2 teaspoons rice wine and soy sauce and cook for 3 minutes. Drain the juices from the beef into the wok and also add the pineapple. Return the beef to the wok and cook until it and the pineapple are heated through. Add the remaining 2 teaspoons sesame oil and give the mixture one or two final stirs. Serve at once.

MARINATED GRILLED PORK CHOPS

*A*nother name for this recipe could well be 'Lazy Pork Chops'. When I am very tired but still hungry for good food, I simply bathe pork chops quickly in a spicy marinade and then almost literally toss them under the grill. They are done in a jiffy and they are delicious with a nice salad which I put together while the chops are grilling. In 15 minutes you have a grand dinner for a lazy (or tired) person. Veal chops work well in this recipe too.

SHOPPING LIST
    1 lb (450 g) pork chops

PREPARATION TIME *5 minutes*

COOKING TIME *7 minutes*

SERVES 4

1 teaspoon dark soy sauce
1 teaspoon light soy sauce
2 teaspoons Chinese rice wine
    or dry sherry
2 teaspoons hoisin sauce
1 teaspoon sesame oil
1 lb (450 g) pork chops

Pre-heat the grill.

Mix together the soy sauces, rice wine, hoisin sauce and sesame oil. Turn the pork chops in the mixture to ensure that they are well coated. Lay the chops on a baking tray and grill for about $3\frac{1}{2}$ minutes on one side, then turn them over and grill the other side for another $3\frac{1}{2}$ minutes or until cooked through. Serve at once.

STIR-FRIED PORK WITH LITCHIS

*P*ork is the 'red meat' of China but, even so, it is almost always served as an accompaniment to other non-meat foods. In this recipe it is paired with litchi fruit. Try to use fresh litchis: their tangy, grape-like flavour goes nicely with that of pork, at once complementing and contrasting with it. Serve over rice.

SHOPPING LIST
1 lb (450 g) lean pork
8 oz (225 g) fresh or tinned litchis
Garlic
Spring onions

PREPARATION TIME *15 minutes (if using tinned litchis); 21 minutes (if using fresh litchis)*

COOKING TIME *3–4 minutes*

SERVES 4–6

1 lb (450 g) lean pork
2 teaspoons light soy sauce
2 teaspoons Chinese rice wine or dry sherry
1 teaspoon sesame oil
2 teaspoons cornflour
8 oz (225 g) fresh or tinned litchis
1½ tablespoons oil (preferably groundnut)
2 tablespoons coarsely chopped garlic
2 tablespoons coarsely chopped spring onions to garnish

Cut the pork into thick ¼ × 2 inch (0.5 × 5 cm) slices and put them into a bowl. Add the soy sauce, rice wine, sesame oil and cornflour and mix well.

If you are using fresh litchis, peel and de-seed them. Set aside. If you are using tinned litchis, drain off the liquid (which you will not need in this recipe) and set the fruit aside.

Heat a wok or large frying-pan, add the oil and garlic and stir-fry for 10 seconds. Put in the pork and continue to stir-fry for 1½ minutes or until it is just cooked through. Add the litchis and continue to stir-fry for another 30 seconds to warm them through. Garnish with the chopped spring onions and serve at once.

STIR-FRIED BEEF WITH ONIONS AND MINT

*S*tir-frying beef is the quick and easy technique *par excellence*. Once the beef is thinly sliced, it congenially combines with any vegetable and cooks very rapidly. Beef, of course, has its own distinct taste, but it has enough character to play nicely with other assertive flavours. Here I borrow from Southeast Asian cuisine and add a touch of refreshing mint (you can substitute fresh basil if you wish). Serve this with rice and you have a wholesome and satisfying one-dish meal.

SHOPPING LIST
1 lb (450 g) lean beef steak
8 oz (225 g) onions
Fresh mint

PREPARATION TIME *15 minutes*

COOKING TIME *7 minutes*

SERVES 4–6

1 lb (450 g) lean beef steak
2 teaspoons light soy sauce
1 teaspoon Chinese rice wine or
    dry sherry
1 teaspoon cornflour
8 oz (225 g) onions
2 tablespoons oil (preferably
    groundnut)
3 tablespoons water
2 tablespoons oyster sauce
Small handful fresh mint leaves

Cut the beef into thick ¼ × 2 inch (0.5 × 5 cm) slices and put them into a bowl. Add the soy sauce, rice wine and cornflour and mix well.

Peel the onions and cut them into thick slices.

Heat a wok or large frying-pan, then pour in the oil. Add the beef and stir-fry for 1 minute to brown. Remove the beef with a slotted spoon and set aside. Add the onions to the wok and stir-fry for 1 minute. Pour in the water and cook for 3 minutes. Drain the juices from the beef into the wok and also add the oyster sauce. Return the beef to the wok and add the mint leaves. Continue to stir-fry for another minute. Serve at once.

MANGO BEEF

*T*his is an example of the New Hong Kong Cuisine, and fast as well. Hong Kong chefs have adapted the exotic mango to new uses, as in this recipe. The soft texture and sensual sweetness of the fruit offer a wonderful contrast and complement to the sturdy familiar virtues of beef. Most of the work involved is preparatory; the cooking takes but a few minutes. Mango Beef is delicious and impressive enough to serve as a main course for either a family or a formal meal.

SHOPPING LIST
1 lb (450 g) lean beef steak
2 fresh mangoes

PREPARATION TIME *15 minutes*

COOKING TIME *3–4 minutes*

SERVES 4–6

1 lb (450 g) lean beef steak
1 tablespoon plus 1 teaspoon
  light soy sauce
3 teaspoons Chinese rice wine
  or dry sherry
2 teaspoons cornflour
2 fresh mangoes
1½ tablespoons oil (preferably
  groundnut)
2 teaspoons dark soy sauce

Cut the beef into thick ¼ × 2 inch (0.5 × 5 cm) slices and put them into a bowl. Add 1 tablespoon of the light soy sauce, 2 teaspoons of the rice wine and the cornflour and mix well.

Peel the mangoes and cut them into thick slices, discarding the stones.

Heat a wok or large frying-pan, then pour in the oil. Add the beef and stir-fry for 2 minutes to brown. Add the remaining 1 teaspoon light soy sauce, the dark soy sauce and the remaining 1 teaspoon rice wine and stir-fry for 30 seconds. Then add the mango slices and heat them through. Give the mixture a final stir and serve at once. The beef should be slightly undercooked as it continues to cook for a short time after it is removed from the wok.

HOT AND TANGY MINCED LAMB

Lamb has a very assertive taste even when it is minced; thus we can use hot and tangy sauces with it and its flavour is still recognisable but in a more palatable form. As is the case with meat sauces in general, this lamb dish, in which the flavours of East and West meet, readily combines with pasta, rice, noodles or even bread to make a quick, easy and substantial meal for four to six people in less than 30 minutes. You can use minced beef instead of lamb if you wish.

SHOPPING LIST
> *1 lb (450 g) minced lamb*
> *Garlic*
> *Fresh root ginger*
> *1 lemon*

PREPARATION TIME *15 minutes*

COOKING TIME *8 minutes*

SERVES 4–6

1 tablespoon oil (preferably groundnut)
1 lb (450 g) minced lamb
3 tablespoons coarsely chopped garlic
2 tablespoons coarsely chopped fresh root ginger
2 tablespoons tomato purée
2 tablespoons sesame paste
1½ tablespoons dark soy sauce
1 tablespoon lemon juice
1 tablespoon chilli bean sauce
2 teaspoons sugar
1 tablespoon Chinese rice wine or dry sherry

Heat a wok or large frying-pan, then add the oil and lamb. Stir-fry for 2 minutes and add the garlic and ginger. Continue cooking for another minute, then stir in the tomato purée, sesame paste, soy sauce, lemon juice, chilli bean sauce, sugar and rice wine. (You will find it quicker, when required to add a number of ingredients at the same time as here, to measure them all into one bowl and add them in one go.) Cook for another 4 minutes. Serve at once.

DO-AHEAD RE-HEATABLE BLACK BEAN SPARERIBS

*B*raised dishes make for quick and easy re-heating. They require a long cooking time in order to bring out their flavour, but once they have been cooked (which can be done even days ahead), the re-heating only improves it. I like to make this dish the night before, then let it cool, remove any fat, cover it and put it in the refrigerator; I then re-heat it when I get home. It also freezes extremely well. The dish is lovely on a cool day served with rice and vegetables.

SHOPPING LIST
  2 lb (900 g) pork spareribs
  Spring onions
  Garlic
  Fresh root ginger
  8 oz (225 g) onions

PREPARATION TIME *15 minutes*

COOKING TIME *50–55 minutes*

SERVES 4–6

2 lb (900 g) pork spareribs
1½ tablespoons oil (preferably groundnut)
3 tablespoons coarsely chopped black beans
3 tablespoons coarsely chopped spring onions
1½ tablespoons finely chopped garlic
1 tablespoon finely chopped fresh root ginger
8 oz (225 g) onions, sliced
5 fl oz (150 ml) Chinese rice wine or dry sherry
5 fl oz (150 ml) water
2 tablespoons dark soy sauce
2 tablespoons light soy sauce
2 teaspoons sugar
1 tablespoon sesame oil

Separate the spareribs into individual ribs and set aside.

Heat a wok or large frying-pan and add the oil. Brown the spareribs, then transfer them to a large heavy saucepan or flameproof casserole. Add the black beans, spring onions, garlic and ginger and stir-fry for 10 seconds. Put in the onions and continue to stir-fry for 2 minutes. Then add the rice wine, water, soy sauces and sugar. Bring the mixture to the boil. Pour this over the spareribs in the saucepan and simmer, covered, for 40 minutes or until the ribs are tender. Uncover and cook over a high heat for 5 minutes to reduce the sauce and finally stir in the sesame oil. Serve at once or allow to cool and re-heat when needed.

SAVOURY CUSTARD WITH PORK, SPRING ONIONS AND OYSTER SAUCE

*T*his sounds complicated but it is quite simple to prepare. Cracking the eggs and chopping the onions take the most time – 5 minutes. The minced meat cooks very quickly. As a child I watched my mother make this dish many times. Served with rice and vegetables, it is a fine, nutritious, family meal.

SHOPPING LIST
  6 eggs
  8 oz (225 g) minced pork
  Spring onions

PREPARATION TIME *12 minutes*

COOKING TIME *12 minutes*

SERVES 4–6

6 eggs, beaten
8 oz (225 g) minced pork
4 tablespoons coarsely chopped
   spring onions
1½ teaspoons salt
2 teaspoons light soy sauce
2 tablespoons oyster sauce
   mixed with 1 teaspoon water

Set a rack in a wok or deep pan. Put in water to a depth of 2½ inches (6 cm) and bring it to a simmer.

Combine the eggs, pork, spring onions, salt and soy sauce and mix well. Pour this into a heatproof dish and set the dish on the rack in the wok. Cover tightly and steam slowly for 12 minutes or until the custard has just set.

Remove the dish from the wok and drizzle with the oyster sauce mixture. Serve at once.

15-MINUTE STEAK

Once in a while, a good steak is just the right thing to prepare. It is certainly quick and easy, and when you add these Chinese seasonings the appeal of the steak, which lends itself well to grilling, is enhanced in many ways. Serve it with rice and your favourite vegetable and you have a wholesome and appetising meal.

SHOPPING LIST
1½ lb (700 g) lean beef steak
Spring onions
Fresh root ginger

PREPARATION TIME *12 minutes*

COOKING TIME *15 minutes*

SERVES 4

1½ lb (700 g) lean beef steak
1 teaspoon salt
½ teaspoon freshly ground
    black pepper
2 teaspoons sesame oil

For the sauce
4 tablespoons coarsely chopped
    spring onions
2 teaspoons coarsely chopped
    fresh root ginger
3 tablespoons oyster sauce
2 tablespoons oil (preferably
    groundnut)

Pre-heat the grill to very hot.

Rub the steak with the salt, pepper and sesame oil. Place the steak on the grill and cook on one side for 7½ minutes. Meanwhile, prepare the spring onions and ginger and place them in a small bowl. Turn the steak over and cook the other side for 7½ minutes (this gives a medium-rare steak). Allow the steak to rest for 10 minutes before slicing.

Just before you are ready to serve, add the oyster sauce to the spring onion mixture. Heat the oil in a small pan until it is smoking and pour this over the sauce mixture. Ladle the sauce over the steak and serve at once.

BARBECUED CHINESE SPARERIBS

Once the preliminary cooking of the ribs is done – and it may be accomplished well ahead of time – this is definitely a quick dish, perfect for a summer evening barbecue. Serve it with salad and perhaps another vegetable, and nice crisp baguettes. These spareribs are made for informal entertaining precisely because most of the work can be done in advance. The slow cooking melts away the fat and helps to tenderise the meat.

SHOPPING LIST
3 lb (1.4 kg) pork spareribs
Garlic
Fresh root ginger

PREPARATION TIME *21 minutes*

COOKING TIME *1½ hours plus 30 minutes*

SERVES 4

3 lb (1.4 kg) pork spareribs
½ teaspoon salt
½ teaspoon coarsely ground
   black pepper

For the barbecue sauce
2 tablespoons light soy sauce
2 tablespoons hoisin sauce
2 tablespoons tomato purée
4 large cloves garlic, peeled
2 tablespoons coarsely chopped
   fresh root ginger
2 tablespoons Chinese rice
   wine or dry sherry
1 tablespoon sugar
1 tablespoon sesame oil
2 teaspoons chilli bean sauce

Pre-heat the oven to gas mark 1, 275°F (140°C).

Place the spareribs in an ovenproof dish. Sprinkle evenly with the salt and pepper. Bake in the oven for 1½ hours.

Combine the barbecue sauce ingredients in a blender and mix for 15–20 seconds or until puréed. Add the sauce to the spareribs and turn to coat evenly. Pre-heat the oven to gas mark 4, 350°F (180°C), and bake the coated spareribs for 30 minutes. Serve at once.

DO-AHEAD RE-HEATABLE LAMB STEW

*Y*ou may have detected a trace of ambivalence on my part concerning lamb: I recognise its virtues but I am not keen about its unmediated taste. Thus I tend to surround it with seasonings and spices that tame its more aggressive aspects, as in this recipe. The long simmering process allows the seasonings to penetrate (and neutralise) the lamb, tenderising it at the same time. You can substitute stewing veal or beef for the lamb if you wish, but remember that stewing beef will take longer to cook. This is a quick and easy dish because it can be made ahead of time and frozen until needed. Serve it with rice and your favourite salad or green vegetable.

SHOPPING LIST
2½ lb (1.25 kg) lamb leg or
shoulder meat
Garlic
Fresh root ginger

PREPARATION TIME *20 minutes*

COOKING TIME *1 hour 35 minutes*

SERVES 4

2½ lb (1.25 kg) lamb leg or
shoulder meat
2 tablespoons oil (preferably
groundnut)
½ teaspoon freshly ground
black pepper
6 cloves garlic, peeled and
crushed
6 slices fresh root ginger
2 pints (1.1 litres) water
2 tablespoons five-spice powder
5 tablespoons sesame paste or
peanut butter
6 tablespoons hoisin sauce
3 tablespoons light soy sauce
3 tablespoons dark soy sauce
4 tablespoons rock or ordinary
sugar
1 tablespoon chilli bean sauce

Cut the lamb into 1 inch (2.5 cm) cubes. Heat a wok or large frying-pan, then add the oil. Add the lamb, sprinkle with the pepper and slowly brown on all sides. Transfer the meat to a large flameproof casserole. Pour all but 1 tablespoon of the oil from the wok. Re-heat the wok and add the garlic and ginger. Stir-fry for 20 seconds and add the rest of the ingredients. Bring the mixture to the boil and pour it over the lamb in the casserole. Simmer for 1½ hours or until the lamb is tender.

STIR-FRIED PORK WITH PINEAPPLE

*P*ork is so distinctly flavoursome that it goes nicely with practically any other assertive ingredient – in this case pineapple. The sweet, slightly acidic fruit blends easily with the pork, while fresh peas add a textural and colourful dimension. Veal may successfully be substituted for the pork if you prefer it. This unusually appetising dish is an ideal centrepiece for a family dinner or a meal for friends *and* it is quick and easy to prepare.

SHOPPING LIST

> *1 lb (450 g) lean pork*
> *1 × 1–1½ lb (450–700 g) fresh pineapple*
> *4 oz (110 g) fresh peas (shelled weight) or frozen peas*
> *Spring onions*

PREPARATION TIME *20 minutes*

COOKING TIME *6 minutes*

SERVES 4–6

1 lb (450 g) lean pork
2 tablespoons light soy sauce
1 teaspoon Chinese rice wine or dry sherry
1 teaspoon salt
2 teaspoons cornflour
1 × 1–1½ lb (450–700 g) fresh pineapple
4 oz (110 g) fresh peas (shelled weight) or frozen peas
1½ tablespoons oil (preferably groundnut)
2 tablespoons coarsely chopped spring onions
2 teaspoons dark soy sauce
2 teaspoons sugar
½ teaspoon cornflour mixed with ½ teaspoon water

Slice the pork into ½ × 3 inch (1 × 7.5 cm) strips and combine them with 1 tablespoon of the light soy sauce, the rice wine, ½ teaspoon of the salt and cornflour in a bowl.

With a sharp knife, remove the skin of the pineapple. Cut the flesh into 1 inch (2.5 cm) cubes, discarding the tough centre core.

If you are using fresh peas, blanch them in boiling water for 2 minutes, drain and set aside. If you are using frozen peas, let them thaw at room temperature.

Heat a wok or large frying-pan, then add the oil, the remaining ½ teaspoon salt and the spring onions. Stir-fry the mixture for 10 seconds. Then add the pork and stir-fry for 1 minute. Put in the pineapple, peas, remaining 1 tablespoon light soy sauce, the dark soy sauce, sugar and cornflour-water mixture. Cook for 2 more minutes or until the pork is just done – it should be firm when it has reached this stage. Serve at once.

VEGETABLES

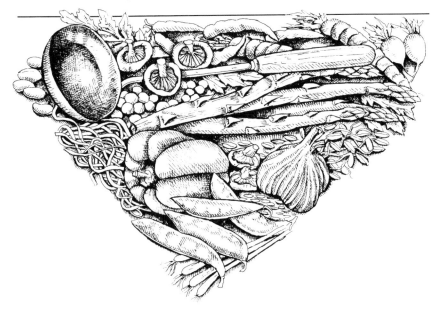

Of all the foods we normally cook, vegetables are undoubtedly the quickest and easiest to prepare. They are generally delicate in flavour and cook rapidly. Thus we need to take great care that we cook them to just the right point or risk losing their natural taste, juice, colour, texture and food value. Properly cooked, vegetables are very nutritious and an extremely important part of the diet.

The Chinese are masters of the art of vegetable cooking, and stir-frying is the perfect technique for vegetables. This rapid method of cooking over high heat retains all of the virtues of the food and leaves it neither raw nor mushy: it is a pleasure to eat. Almost all vegetables may be stir-fried, as the recipes here indicate. Follow them but adapt them to your own taste. Use vegetables in season imaginatively and creatively.

QUICK BEAN CURD IN SPICY CHILLI SAUCE

*T*his is my version of the classic Sichuan bean curd dish. I have simplified the process but it is as colourful and tasty as the original. Serve it to accompany a main meal with rice. Left-overs from this dish can be put into stock to make a quick soup.

SHOPPING LIST
> *Garlic*
> *Fresh root ginger*
> *Spring onions*
> *1 lb (450 g) firm bean curd*

PREPARATION TIME *11 minutes*

COOKING TIME *9 minutes*

SERVES 4–6

1 tablespoon oil (preferably groundnut)
1 tablespoon coarsely chopped garlic
2 teaspoons finely chopped fresh root ginger
3 tablespoons coarsely chopped spring onions
3 tablespoons water
1 tablespoon yellow bean sauce
1 tablespoon tomato purée
2 teaspoons chilli bean sauce
2 teaspoons dark soy sauce
2 teaspoons sugar
2 teaspoons sesame oil
1 lb (450 g) firm bean curd

Heat a wok or large frying-pan and add the oil, garlic, ginger and spring onions. Stir-fry the mixture for 30 seconds, then add all the remaining ingredients except the bean curd. Simmer the mixture for 5 minutes. While the sauce is simmering, cut the bean curd into ½ inch (1 cm) dice. Add the diced bean curd to the sauce and simmer for another 3 minutes. Serve at once.

CHILLI CON CARNE.

1 lb steak mince	Tomato Puree
2 onions (MED) chopped.	KIDNEY Beans
2 peppers sliced	Mushrooms.
1 tin tomatoes — chopped	1/4 lb.

1. drain tomato juice into cup.
2. add 1 heaped teaspoon chilli powder
   and add to tomato juice & stir
3. 1 teaspoon garlic powder / salt add
   to cup
4. 1 level teaspoon cayenne pepper
   added to cup

Brown mince - add onions - stir for
5 MINS - add tube of tomato puree -
add chopped tomatoes (remove core) -
add cup of mixture to pot. - add
peppers - add mushrooms - small tin of
washed BAKED Beans -

Great Universal

Where value and service mean a great deal

ORDER FORM

IF YOU HAVE CHANGED YOUR
ADDRESS SINCE YOUR LAST ORDER
PLEASE MARK 'X' IN THIS BOX ▶

REFERENCE
NUMBER

☐☐☐☐ ☐☐☐☐ DATE

YOUR NAME _____ (PLEASE USE BLOCK CAPITALS)

ADDRESS _____

_____ POSTCODE _____

TELEPHONE NO. _____
(STD CODE ESSENTIAL) ☐☐☐☐☐☐

DELIVERY TO AN ALTERNATIVE ADDRESS
IF YOU REQUIRE THIS SERVICE, PLEASE ENTER THE
NAME AND ADDRESS BELOW IN BLOCK CAPITALS.

1. A separate form must be used for each different address.

2. IMPORTANT. When ordering wines and spirits see your catalogue for special instructions.

Name _____

Address _____

Postcode _____

Telephone. No. _____

PLEASE STATE CAREFULLY

- The correct PAGE/LEAFLET NUMBER AND CATALOGUE NUMBER for each item.
- The PRICE FOR ONE item, even when more than one is required.
- Don't forget to enter YDS. FT. METRES. SETS etc. where applicable.
- The SIZE and/or COLOUR where there is a choice.

	PAGE OR LEAFLET NUMBER	CATALOGUE NUMBER	PRICE EACH £	PRICE EACH p	HOW MANY	YDS. FT. METRES, SETS.,ETC.	SIZE	COLOUR	DESCRIPTION
1									
2									
3									
4									
5									
6									
7									
8									
9									
10									

You can always request stationery when ordering goods through HOTLINE

Simmer for 45 minutes – add
a large tin of KIDNEY BEANS
(washed & drained) for a ½hr

Serve with Boiled Rice (enty Dn

Great Universal
Where value and service mean a great deal

ORDER FORM

YOUR NAME _____ (PLEASE USE BLOCK CAPITALS)

ADDRESS _____

_____ POSTCODE _____

TELEPHONE NO. _____ (STD CODE ESSENTIAL)

REFERENCE NUMBER

DATE _____

DELIVERY TO AN ALTERNATIVE ADDRESS
IF YOU REQUIRE THIS SERVICE, PLEASE ENTER THE NAME AND ADDRESS BELOW IN BLOCK CAPITALS.

Name _____

Address _____

Postcode _____

Telephone. No. _____

1. A separate form must be used for each different address.

2. IMPORTANT. When ordering wines and spirits see your catalogue for special instructions.

PLEASE STATE CAREFULLY

- The correct PAGE/LEAFLET NUMBER AND CATALOGUE NUMBER for each item.
- The PRICE FOR ONE item, even when more than one is required
- Don't forget to enter YDS, FT. METRES, SETS etc, where applicable.
- The SIZE and/or COLOUR where there is a choice.

	PAGE OR LEAFLET NUMBER	CATALOGUE NUMBER	PRICE EACH £	p	HOW MANY	YDS. FT. METRES, SETS, ETC.	SIZE	COLOUR	DESCRIPTION
1									
2									
3									
4									
5									
6									
7									
8									
9									
10									

You can always request stationery when ordering goods through HOTLINE

RED-COOKED WINTER VEGETABLES

*R*ed-cooking is usually reserved for meats – simmering them in a rich red sauce of Chinese spices. The technique works as well, however, with winter root vegetables, making a quick tasty stew. On a cold winter evening, this dish goes perfectly with meat or poultry and a salad.

SHOPPING LIST
  1 lb (450 g) carrots
  8 oz (225 g) turnips
  Garlic
  Fresh root ginger

PREPARATION TIME *10 minutes*

COOKING TIME *12 minutes*

SERVES 4

1 lb (450 g) carrots
8 oz (225 g) turnips
1 tablespoon oil (preferably groundnut)
2 cloves garlic, peeled and crushed
2 teaspoons coarsely chopped fresh root ginger
3 tablespoons hoisin sauce
1 tablespoon dark soy sauce
2 teaspoons sugar
5 fl oz (150 ml) water

Peel and cut the carrots into 1 inch (2.5 cm) pieces. Peel the turnips and cut them into 1 inch (2.5 cm) cubes.

Heat a wok or large frying-pan, then add the oil, garlic and ginger. Stir-fry for 10 seconds and add the carrots, hoisin sauce, soy sauce, sugar and water. Cover and cook over a high heat for 8 minutes. Then add the turnips and continue to cook for another 3 minutes or until all the vegetables are tender. There should be very little sauce left. Turn on to a platter and serve at once.

STIR-FRIED EGGS AND CORN WITH SPRING ONIONS AND GINGER

I often make this dish when I am hungry and need a sustaining nutritious meal in a hurry. Corn has made its way from the West to China, and in Hong Kong especially you will find it a popular food. As this delicious combination indicates, Chinese chefs have thoroughly integrated corn into the Chinese cuisine. You can substitute fresh or frozen peas for the corn if you wish.

SHOPPING LIST
  1 lb (450 g) fresh sweetcorn on the cob or 10 oz (275 g) frozen sweetcorn
  Spring onions
  Fresh root ginger
  4 eggs

PREPARATION TIME *10 minutes*

COOKING TIME *5 minutes*

SERVES 4

1 lb (450 g) fresh sweetcorn on the cob or 10 oz (275 g) frozen sweetcorn
1 tablespoon oil (preferably groundnut)
3 tablespoons coarsely chopped spring onions
2 teaspoons finely chopped fresh root ginger
1 teaspoon salt
4 eggs, lightly beaten

If you are using fresh corn on the cob, clean it and remove the kernels with a sharp knife or cleaver – you should end up with about 10 oz (275 g). Set it aside. If you are using frozen corn, place it in a bowl and let it thaw at room temperature.

Heat a wok or large frying-pan, then add the oil. Add the spring onions, ginger and salt and stir-fry for 10 seconds. Add the corn and continue to stir-fry for 2 minutes. Finally, turn the heat to medium, add the eggs and continue to cook for another 2 minutes. Serve at once.

STIR-FRIED BROAD BEANS WITH HAM AND SPRING ONIONS

Shanghai-style and quick and easy, this dish can be served as an accompaniment but is substantial enough to stand on its own. With another vegetable dish, it makes for a light nutritious meal. Fresh or frozen peas or sweetcorn may be used instead of the broad beans.

SHOPPING LIST
  *1½ lb (700 g) fresh or 1 lb
    (450 g) frozen broad beans*
  *3 tablespoons finely chopped
    Parma ham*
  Spring onions

PREPARATION TIME *10 minutes*

COOKING TIME *5–6 minutes*

SERVES 4–6

1½ lb (700 g) fresh or 1 lb
  (450 g) frozen broad beans
Salt
1½ tablespoons oil (preferably
  groundnut)
3 tablespoons finely chopped
  Parma ham
4 tablespoons coarsely chopped
  spring onions
2 teaspoons sesame oil

If you are using fresh broad beans, shell them and blanch for 4 minutes in boiling salted water. Drain and set aside. If you are using frozen broad beans, let them thaw at room temperature.

Heat a wok or large frying-pan, then add the oil. Add the ham and stir-fry for 1 minute. Then add the broad beans and continue to stir-fry for 3 minutes. Add the spring onions and 1 teaspoon salt and stir-fry for a further 1 minute. Stir in the sesame oil and serve at once.

OYSTER SAUCE ASPARAGUS

*W*hen asparagus is in season, enjoy it as much as possible; it is a superb vegetable, the favourite of many people. I never tire of it and I am sad when its season ends. Here I combine it with a savoury oyster sauce. This has a robust flavour which the asparagus readily accepts and the result is as satisfying as a meat and vegetable dish. Serve it by itself or as part of a family meal.

SHOPPING LIST
  1½ lb (700 g) fresh asparagus
  Garlic
  Spring onions

PREPARATION TIME *15 minutes*

COOKING TIME *5 minutes*

SERVES 4

1½ lb (700 g) fresh asparagus
1½ tablespoons oil (preferably groundnut)
2 tablespoons thinly sliced garlic
2 tablespoons coarsely chopped spring onions
½ teaspoon salt
Pinch of sugar
4 tablespoons water
2 tablespoons oyster sauce

Cut the asparagus into 3 inch (7.5 cm) lengths and set aside.

Heat a wok or large frying-pan and add the oil. Then add the garlic and spring onions and stir-fry for 30 seconds. Add the asparagus, salt and sugar and stir-fry for 1 minute. Add the water, cover and cook for 3 minutes. Then add the oyster sauce, stir to mix well and serve at once.

Green Rice (page 120)
Bean Sauce Noodles (page 116)

STIR-FRIED FENNEL WITH GARLIC

*D*uring my frequent visits to England I like to cook 'Chinese/English' for friends. On such occasions I always prepare vegetables in season. I recently discovered that fennel is delicious stir-fried. I had, of course, long been familiar with its liquorice-flavoured herbal qualities. But, even though I knew it as a popular dish in the South of France and in Italy, I had never prepared it as a vegetable dish. Serve it with one of the quick grilled chop recipes and you have a very satisfying meal.

SHOPPING LIST
> *1 lb (450 g) fennel*
> *8 oz (225 g) red peppers*
> *Garlic*

PREPARATION TIME *10 minutes*

COOKING TIME *6 minutes*

SERVES 4–6

1 lb (450 g) fennel
8 oz (225 g) red peppers
1½ tablespoons oil (preferably groundnut)
4 cloves garlic, peeled and crushed
1 teaspoon salt
2 tablespoons water

Trim the fennel and quarter it, separating the layers. De-seed the peppers and cut them into strips.

Heat a wok or large frying-pan, then add the oil, garlic and salt. Stir-fry for 10 seconds and add the fennel, peppers and water. Continue to stir-fry for 5 minutes or until the vegetables are cooked through, if necessary adding more water to keep them from burning. Serve at once.

Mango Fool (page 126)
Litchis with Papaya Sauce (page 126)

Stir-Fried Peas with Fresh Coriander and Spring Onions

*B*ecause of their sweetness and succulent texture, peas are always popular. Here I have enhanced their virtues with some spirited seasonings to make a quick, easy and tasty vegetable dish. Try also serving it at room temperature as part of a buffet.

SHOPPING LIST
> *1 lb (450 g) fresh peas (shelled*
> *weight) or frozen peas*
> *Fresh coriander*
> *Spring onions*
> *Garlic*

PREPARATION TIME *11 minutes (if using fresh peas); 5 minutes (if using frozen peas)*

COOKING TIME *4 minutes*

SERVES 4–6

1 lb (450 g) fresh peas (shelled weight) or frozen peas
1 tablespoon oil (preferably groundnut)
2 tablespoons finely chopped fresh coriander
2 tablespoons finely chopped spring onions
2 teaspoons finely chopped garlic
1 teaspoon sugar
1 teaspoon salt
½ teaspoon freshly ground white pepper
2 teaspoons sesame oil

If you are using fresh peas, blanch them in boiling water for 2 minutes, drain and set aside. If you are using frozen peas, let them thaw at room temperature.

Heat a wok or large frying-pan, then add the oil. Add the peas and stir-fry for 30 seconds, then add the coriander, spring onions, garlic, sugar, salt and pepper and continue to stir-fry for 3 minutes or until the peas are cooked. Add the sesame oil, give the mixture a final stir and serve at once.

POTATOES WITH A FRESH CORIANDER, SPRING ONION AND SESAME OIL DRESSING

*P*otatoes are known in China but they are not a popular food. As Western as I am, however, I have long since discovered and learned to love the virtues of this wholesome vegetable. I especially like new potatoes. The potato's one flaw is that it is rather bland; however, it is also congenially receptive to lively seasonings, as in this recipe. The Chinese spices and herbs lend the potatoes an exotic touch. This easy-to-prepare dish will gracefully accompany a meat dish (particularly a grilled one) at any gathering, formal or informal.

SHOPPING LIST
1 lb (450 g) small new potatoes
Fresh coriander
Spring onions

PREPARATION TIME *10 minutes*

COOKING TIME *15 minutes*

SERVES 4–6

Salt
1 lb (450 g) small new potatoes
2 tablespoons white rice vinegar
3 tablespoons finely chopped fresh coriander
3 tablespoons finely chopped spring onions
1 tablespoon sesame oil
2 teaspoons oil (preferably groundnut)

Scrub the potatoes but do not peel them. Cook them in boiling salted water for about 15 minutes or until they are just cooked through. Drain them thoroughly and put them into a serving bowl.

In another small bowl, mix 1 teaspoon salt with the vinegar and combine with the coriander and spring onions. Slowly beat in the oils, pour over the potatoes, toss well and serve at once.

OYSTER SAUCE BEAN CURD

Bean curd (*tofu*) is an inexpensive, very nutritious food that is also delicious when combined with appropriate seasonings and properly cooked. Here oyster sauce and pan-frying create a most enjoyable bean curd dish.

SHOPPING LIST
1 lb (450 g) firm bean curd
Garlic

PREPARATION TIME *9 minutes*

COOKING TIME *12 minutes*

SERVES 4

1 lb (450 g) firm bean curd
3 tablespoons oil (preferably groundnut)
2 cloves garlic, peeled and crushed
3 tablespoons oyster sauce
2 tablespoons water
1 teaspoon sugar
2 teaspoons sesame oil

Cut the bean curd into 1 inch (2.5 cm) cubes.

Heat a wok or large frying-pan, then add the oil. Slowly fry the bean curd on each side until it is golden-brown – you may have to do this in several batches. Remove it from the wok and drain on kitchen paper.

Pour off from the wok all but 1 tablespoon of oil. Re-heat the wok and remaining oil, add the garlic and stir-fry for 10 seconds. Then add the oyster sauce, water, sugar and sesame oil. Bring to a simmer, return the bean curd cubes to the wok and heat them through. Serve at once.

FAST MANGE-TOUT WITH MUSHROOMS

These mange-tout (or Chinese peas, as they are sometimes called) are refreshingly different in that the crisp edible pod is so tasty a complement to the green peas themselves – they are among my very favourite vegetables, and so quick and easy to prepare. Combined with the softer, meatier mushrooms and enhancing seasonings, they make a splendid vegetable dish in less than 20 minutes.

SHOPPING LIST
    8 oz (225 g) small mushrooms
    1 lb (450 g) mange-tout

PREPARATION TIME *10 minutes*

COOKING TIME *7 minutes*

SERVES 4–6

1½ tablespoons oil (preferably
    groundnut)
8 oz (225 g) small mushrooms,
    wiped
1 lb (450 g) mange-tout,
    trimmed
1 teaspoon sugar
2 teaspoons dark soy sauce
2 teaspoons sesame oil

Heat a wok or large frying-pan and add the oil and mushrooms. Stir-fry for 4 minutes, then add the mange-tout, sugar, soy sauce and sesame oil. Continue to stir-fry for another 2 minutes. Serve at once.

STIR-FRIED GINGER SPINACH

*T*he hardest part of this recipe is cleaning the spinach. After that, it is quick, easy and ginger-delicious all the way!

SHOPPING LIST
    1½ lb (700 g) fresh spinach
    Fresh root ginger

PREPARATION TIME *7 minutes*

COOKING TIME *5 minutes*

SERVES 4–6

1½ lb (700 g) fresh spinach
1 tablespoon oil (preferably
    groundnut)
2 tablespoons finely shredded
    fresh root ginger
1 teaspoon salt
1 teaspoon sugar
2 teaspoons sesame oil

Remove the stalks from the spinach leaves. Wash the leaves well in several changes of cold water.

Heat a wok or large frying-pan, then add the oil, ginger and salt. Stir-fry the mixture for 20 seconds. Add the spinach and stir-fry for 2 minutes to coat the leaves thoroughly with the mixture. When the spinach has wilted to about a third of its original size, add the sugar and sesame oil. Continue to stir-fry for another 2 minutes. Serve hot or cold.

HOT AND TANGY COURGETTES

Courgettes are easy to prepare and can be elevated from their bland natural state into something quite impressively tangy, as in this recipe. They are made spicy and colourful here, and can grace any table as an accompaniment to a main course. They may also be served at room temperature for a warm summer evening meal.

SHOPPING LIST
1½ lb (700 g) courgettes
Garlic

PREPARATION TIME *9 minutes*

COOKING TIME *5 minutes*

SERVES 4–6

1½ lb (700 g) courgettes, trimmed
1 tablespoon oil (preferably groundnut)
2 teaspoons chilli bean sauce
1 tablespoon coarsely chopped garlic
1 tablespoon coarsely chopped black beans
2 tablespoons white rice vinegar
1 tablespoon Chinese rice wine or dry sherry
3 tablespoons water
2 teaspoons sesame oil

Cut the courgettes into 1 inch (2.5 cm) thick slices.

Heat a wok or large frying-pan, then add the oil, chilli bean sauce, garlic and black beans and stir-fry for 10 seconds. Add the courgettes and stir-fry for 2 minutes. Then add the vinegar, rice wine and water and continue to cook for 2 minutes. Finally, stir in the sesame oil and serve.

POTATOES IN
CURRY-COCONUT STEW

*T*his is essentially a potato stew, but one given new dimensions by the savoury and exotic seasonings. Moreover, it is ready in little more than 30 minutes, and if it is more convenient you can peel the potatoes up to 4 hours in advance and leave them, covered with water, in the refrigerator until you want to cook them. You can also substitute carrots or turnips for the potatoes. The rich flavour and substantial nature of this dish make for a very satisfying vegetarian meal. Serve it with a green vegetable or salad.

SHOPPING LIST
1½ lb (700 g) potatoes
8 oz (225 g) onions
Garlic
Fresh root ginger

PREPARATION TIME *19 minutes*

COOKING TIME *17 minutes*

SERVES 4–6

1½ lb (700 g) potatoes
8 oz (225 g) onions
1½ tablespoons oil (preferably groundnut)
2 tablespoons coarsely chopped garlic
1 tablespoon coarsely chopped fresh root ginger
3 tablespoons curry paste
15 fl oz (400 ml) tinned coconut milk
4 tablespoons water
1 tablespoon light soy sauce
2 teaspoons sugar

Peel the potatoes and cut them into 1 inch (2.5 cm) cubes. Peel and coarsely chop the onions.

Heat a wok or large frying-pan, then add the oil, onions, garlic and ginger. Stir-fry the mixture for 1 minute. Then add the potatoes, curry paste, coconut milk, water, soy sauce and sugar. Bring the mixture to a simmer, cover and cook for 15 minutes or until the potatoes are tender. Serve at once.

HOT AND SPICY
STIR-FRIED CABBAGE

Cabbage has a distinct but delicate flavour that adapts well to a wide range of seasonings. Because it is a 'cold' vegetable, I believe that it needs the assistance or enhancement of something like zesty Sichuan spices, as in this recipe. This easy-to-make dish makes a delicious accompaniment to all types of main course. With rice and another quick vegetable dish, it may also serve as a part of a vegetarian meal. You can use Chinese leaves instead of cabbage if you wish.

SHOPPING LIST

    1 lb (450 g) cabbage
    Garlic
    Fresh root ginger

PREPARATION TIME *8 minutes*

COOKING TIME *5 minutes*

SERVES 4–6

Salt
1 lb (450 g) cabbage
1½ tablespoons oil (preferably groundnut)
2 tablespoons coarsely chopped garlic
1 tablespoon coarsely chopped fresh root ginger
1 tablespoon dark soy sauce
1 tablespoon oyster sauce
2 teaspoons chilli bean sauce
2 teaspoons sesame oil

Bring a large pan of salted water to the boil. Cut the cabbage into strips about ½ inch (1 cm) wide. Blanch the cabbage in the boiling water for 2 minutes – this removes any harshness of flavour and brings out the sweet taste. Drain thoroughly.

Heat a wok or large frying-pan, then add the oil, garlic and ginger. Stir-fry for about 10 seconds and add the cabbage. Continue stir-frying for 2 minutes, then add the sauces and sesame oil and cook for another 2 minutes. Serve at once.

BRIGHT PEPPER AND GREEN BEAN STIR-FRY

*R*ed peppers and green beans, nicely seasoned, combine to form a colourful blend of tastes and textures, a nutritious and attractive salad appropriate for any meal: very quick, very easy and very satisfying. This dish is also good served at room temperature.

SHOPPING LIST

8 oz (225 g) red peppers
Garlic
8 oz (225 g) French beans

PREPARATION TIME *15 minutes*

COOKING TIME *7 minutes*

SERVES 4–6

8 oz (225 g) red peppers
1½ tablespoons oil (preferably groundnut)
2 tablespoons coarsely chopped garlic
1½ teaspoons salt
8 oz (225 g) French beans, trimmed and left whole
1 teaspoon sugar
2 tablespoons water

De-seed the peppers and cut them into strips.

Heat a wok or large frying-pan, then add the oil. Add the garlic, salt, peppers and beans and stir-fry for 2 minutes. Then add the sugar and water and continue to cook for another 4 minutes or until the vegetables are tender. Serve at once.

CHINESE-STYLE OMELETTE

A simple omelette is one of life's pleasures. It is an ideal food at the end of a long day when you are hungry but don't have much time or energy to devote to preparing a meal. But it must be done with care and imagination. I often prepare this Chinese-style omelette while my rice is heating. Add a salad or a favourite green vegetable and you have a very quick and quite refreshing meal in 15–20 minutes.

SHOPPING LIST
8 oz (225 g) bean sprouts
6 eggs
Spring onions
Fresh coriander

PREPARATION TIME *9 minutes*

COOKING TIME *4 minutes*

SERVES 4

1½ tablespoons oil (preferably groundnut)
1½ teaspoons salt
8 oz (225 g) bean sprouts
6 eggs, lightly beaten
4 tablespoons coarsely chopped spring onions
2 tablespoons coarsely chopped fresh coriander
2 tablespoons oyster sauce mixed with 1 tablespoon water

Heat a wok or large frying-pan and add the oil, salt and bean sprouts. Cook for 1 minute and pour in the beaten eggs and add the spring onions and fresh coriander. Allow to cook for 2 minutes, then with a spatula turn half of the omelette up over the other half. It should be moist but cooked through. Drizzle with the oyster sauce mixture and serve at once.

7

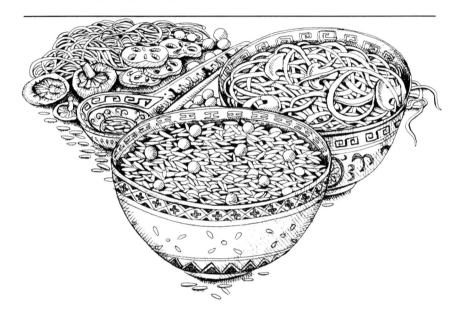

ΠOODLES & RICE

*N*oodles are among the quickest foods to cook, and rice, while it takes a little longer, re-heats nicely and so can be prepared in advance. Indeed, some rice dishes require re-heated rice. Asian cities are filled with street stalls and wagons that sell the area's 'fast food', rice and noodles, for a quick meal or snack. These are warming and satisfying dishes, easy to serve and as easy to make. They are the perfect base for a one-dish meal.

Some of the preparation for a rice dish can be done ahead of time, and once the rice is made the rest of the dish is rapidly put together. In most of the noodle recipes I use rice noodles for convenience. These keep indefinitely in their dried state, needing no refrigeration. They require very little cooking – not even the short boiling that egg noodles and pasta need – and can be placed directly into the dish being prepared. If time is really at a premium, rely on rice noodles.

Many of the dishes in this section may serve as part of a larger meal or simply as a light meal in themselves – rice and pasta are quite satisfying. Some of the recipes can be served at room temperature for a buffet or as exotic picnic fare. Use them creatively and imaginatively, to suit your own taste and needs.

Bean Sauce Noodles

*T*his northern Chinese original is one of the quickest and easiest meals you can make – cooking the noodles accounts for most of the time involved, and once they are covered with boiling water you can leave them. While waiting, you could get up a nice salad and slice some fruit for dessert. Instead of pork and flat rice noodles you could use minced beef and egg noodles (see page 17 for cooking instructions) to make this dish.

SHOPPING LIST
    12 oz (350 g) minced pork
    Spring onions

PREPARATION TIME *23 minutes*

COOKING TIME *6 minutes*

SERVES 4–6

8 oz (225 g) flat rice noodles
1 tablespoon light soy sauce
2 teaspoons sesame oil
1 tablespoon oil (preferably groundnut)
12 oz (350 g) minced pork
5 tablespoons yellow bean sauce
2 teaspoons sugar
6 spring onions, coarsely chopped

Bring a large saucepan of water to the boil, remove it from the heat and add the rice noodles. Leave to stand for about 15 minutes. While the noodles are soaking, prepare the rest of the ingredients.

Drain the noodles and toss them with the soy sauce and sesame oil. Heat a wok or large frying-pan and add the oil and pork. Stir-fry for 2 minutes, breaking up any clumps of meat. Then add the yellow bean sauce and sugar and cook for 3 minutes more. Stir in the spring onions.

Place the noodles on a platter, ladle the sauce over and serve.

SPICY RICE NOODLES
WITH MUSSELS

*T*his dish is useful for entertaining a large group of friends at short notice. Only the careful cleaning of the mussels takes any time; the rest of the preparation is very quick. Make sure that all the mussels are firmly closed before cooking: throw away any that do not close up when touched or that have damaged shells. You can substitute prawns or clams for mussels, but whatever seafood you use will result in a tasty and substantial dish that, with rice noodles, for example, makes a complete and satisfying meal.

SHOPPING LIST
    Garlic
    Spring onions
    2 lb (900 g) fresh mussels

PREPARATION TIME *23 minutes*

COOKING TIME *8–9 minutes plus 15 minutes' standing time*

SERVES 4–6

8 oz (225 g) rice noodles, rice vermicelli or rice sticks
2 tablespoons oil (preferably groundnut)
1 tablespoon black beans
2 tablespoons coarsely chopped garlic
2 tablespoons coarsely chopped spring onions
2 lb (900 g) fresh mussels, well scrubbed
1 tablespoon Chinese rice wine or dry sherry
1 tablespoon yellow bean sauce
2 teaspoons chilli bean sauce

Bring a large saucepan of water to the boil, remove from heat and add the rice noodles. Leave to stand for about 15 minutes, then drain well.

Heat a wok or large frying-pan and add the oil, black beans (leave these whole), garlic and spring onions. Stir-fry for 20 seconds and add the mussels, rice wine, yellow bean sauce and chilli bean sauce. Continue to cook for 5 minutes or until all the mussels have opened. Discard any which have not opened. Add the rice noodles and cook for another 2 minutes, mixing well. Give the dish a final stir and serve at once.

Rice Noodles with Broccoli

*T*his recipe takes advantage of the quick cooking characteristics of rice noodles. Boiled for about 2 minutes and then combined with the blanched broccoli for another few minutes, the noodles make a delectable vegetarian dish for one or two people. For a more spicy flavour add 2 teaspoons chilli bean sauce when you add the other sauces. Any left-overs can be re-heated very easily by stir-frying.

Shopping List

    1 lb (450 g) broccoli
    12 oz (350 g) thin dried rice noodles
    Garlic
    Spring onions

Preparation Time *15 minutes*

Cooking Time *8 minutes*

Serves 4–6

Salt
1 lb (450 g) broccoli
12 oz (350 g) thin dried rice noodles
1½ tablespoons oil (preferably groundnut)
2 tablespoons coarsely chopped garlic
2 tablespoons coarsely chopped spring onions
3 tablespoons water
2 tablespoons oyster sauce
1 tablespoon dark soy sauce
2 teaspoons sesame oil

Fill a large pan with water, add salt to taste and bring to the boil. Separate the broccoli heads into small florets, and peel and slice the stems. Blanch the broccoli pieces in the boiling water for 4 minutes.

Place the rice noodles in a large heatproof bowl. Drain the hot water from the blanched broccoli over the rice noodles and immerse the broccoli pieces in cold water. Drain the broccoli thoroughly and set aside.

Let the noodles stand in the hot water for 2 minutes, then drain. Heat a wok or large frying-pan and add the oil, garlic and spring onions. Stir-fry for 20 seconds. Stir in the drained rice noodles and broccoli and continue to stir-fry for 1 minute. Then add the water, oyster sauce, soy sauce and sesame oil and cook for 2 minutes. Turn the mixture on to a platter and serve at once.

ELIZABETH CHONG'S NOODLE SALAD

As one of Australia's leading teachers of Chinese cookery, Elizabeth Chong is very much worth listening to. And because she leads so busy a professional life – teaching, travelling, demonstrating and writing – she is an authority on quick, easy and delicious meals. This recipe, which I have adapted from one of her own, represents the best of good food, even though it is so simple to prepare. Serve the salad on a bed of lettuce surrounded with sliced tomatoes as an unusual side dish – most refreshing on a warm day!

SHOPPING LIST
12 oz (350 g) bean sprouts
Spring onions

PREPARATION TIME *15 minutes*

COOKING TIME *2 minutes*

SERVES 4–6

6 oz (175 g) bean thread noodles
1 tablespoon oil (preferably groundnut)
2 teaspoons salt
12 oz (350 g) bean sprouts
6 spring onions, finely shredded
1½ teaspoons chilli bean sauce
1½ tablespoons white rice vinegar
1 tablespoon light soy sauce
2 teaspoons sesame oil

Soak the noodles in a large bowl of warm water for 5 minutes. (While they are soaking, prepare the other ingredients.) When the noodles are soft, drain them well and cut them into 3 inch (7.5 cm) lengths using scissors or a knife.

Heat a wok or large frying-pan and add the oil, salt, bean sprouts and spring onions. Stir-fry for 10 seconds, then add the chilli bean sauce, rice vinegar, soy sauce, sesame oil and noodles and cook for 1 minute. Allow the mixture to cool, then refrigerate. Serve cold as an accompaniment to grilled or cold meats.

GREEN RICE

*T*his dish is not really green but is attractively dotted with the green of peas, coriander and spring onions and redolent of their flavours and pungency. You can speed up the preparation by boiling the rice in advance – store it, well covered, in the refrigerator until you need it. Serve Green Rice at room temperature as a tasty rice salad or as part of a meal.

SHOPPING LIST
> *8 oz (225 g) fresh peas (shelled*
> *weight) or frozen peas*
> *Garlic*
> *Fresh coriander*
> *Spring onions*

PREPARATION TIME *rice – 5 minutes;*
> *Green Rice – 15 minutes*

COOKING TIME *rice – 25 minutes;*
> *Green Rice – 7–8 minutes*

SERVES 4–6

15 fl oz (400 ml) long-grain rice
1½ pints (900 ml) water
8 oz (225 g) fresh peas (shelled
    weight) or frozen peas
1 tablespoon oil (preferably
    groundnut)
1 tablespoon coarsely chopped
    garlic
3 tablespoons finely chopped
    fresh coriander
6 tablespoons finely chopped
    spring onions
2 teaspoons salt

Put the rice in a heavy pan with the water and bring it to the boil. Continue boiling for about 10 minutes or until most of the surface liquid has evaporated. The surface of the rice should have small indentations and look rather like a pitted crater. At this point, cover the pan with a very tight-fitting lid, turn the heat as low as possible and let the rice cook undisturbed for 15 minutes more. Remove from the heat and allow to cool thoroughly – the colder the rice, the better it stir-fries.

If you are using fresh peas, blanch them in boiling water for 2 minutes, then drain and set aside. If you are using frozen peas, let them thaw at room temperature.

Heat a wok or large frying-pan, then add the oil. Add the garlic and stir-fry for 10 seconds. Add the rice and continue to stir-fry for 3 minutes. Now add coriander, spring onions, peas and salt and stir-fry for 2 minutes. Serve at once or allow to cool and serve at room temperature.

HOT AND SPICY RICE WITH BEEF

*R*ice dishes need not be bland, as the aromatic seasonings and spices in this recipe prove. This can be a one-dish meal; simply serve it with a favourite salad or vegetable. Speed up the preparation by boiling the rice in advance – store it, well covered, in the refrigerator until you need it.

SHOPPING LIST
> *1 lb (450 g) minced beef*
> *Garlic*
> *Fresh root ginger*
> *Spring onions*

PREPARATION TIME *rice – 5 minutes;*
> *Hot and Spicy Rice – 7 minutes*

COOKING TIME *rice – 25 minutes;*
> *Hot and Spicy Rice – 10 minutes*

SERVES 4–6

15 fl oz (400 ml) long-grain rice
1½ pints (900 ml) water
4 tablespoons oil (preferably groundnut)
2 teaspoons salt
1 lb (450 g) minced beef
2 tablespoons coarsely chopped garlic
1 tablespoon coarsely chopped fresh root ginger
2 teaspoons chilli bean sauce
1 teaspoon curry paste or powder
3 tablespoons coarsely chopped spring onions

Put the rice in a heavy pan with the water and bring it to the boil. Continue boiling for about 10 minutes or until most of the surface liquid has evaporated. The surface of the rice should have small indentations and look rather like a pitted crater. At this point, cover the pan with a very tight-fitting lid, turn the heat as low as possible and let the rice cook undisturbed for 15 minutes more. Remove from the heat and allow to cool.

Heat a wok or large frying-pan and add 2 tablespoons of the oil and the salt. Add the beef and stir-fry for 4 minutes, stirring well to break up any clumps of meat. Remove the cooked meat from the wok and set aside. Drain the oil from the wok. Re-heat the wok and add the remaining 2 tablespoons oil. Then add the garlic, ginger, chilli bean sauce and curry paste or powder and stir-fry for 30 seconds. Now add the cooked rice and beef and the spring onions and continue to stir-fry for another 5 minutes. Serve at once or allow to cool and serve at room temperature.

MINCED PORK, PEA AND RICE CASSEROLE

*T*his is a typical Chinese dish, designed to comfort, to satisfy, to relax one's body and soul. It re-heats very well (when it is perhaps even tastier) and is a meal in itself. Serve it with a favourite salad and you have a splendid, complete meal.

SHOPPING LIST
> *8 oz (225 g) fresh peas (shelled weight) or frozen peas*
> *1 lb (450 g) minced pork*
> *Spring onions*

PREPARATION TIME *15 minutes*

COOKING TIME *25 minutes*

SERVES 4

15 fl oz (400 ml) long-grain rice
1½ pints (900 ml) water
8 oz (225 g) fresh peas (shelled weight) or frozen peas
1½ tablespoons oil (preferably groundnut)
1 lb (450 g) minced pork
1 tablespoon light soy sauce
1 tablespoon dark soy sauce
1 tablespoon oyster sauce
½ teaspoon salt
1 tablespoon Chinese rice wine or dry sherry
3 tablespoons finely chopped spring onions

Put the rice in a heavy pan with the water and bring it to the boil. Continue boiling for about 10 minutes or until most of the surface liquid has evaporated. The surface of the rice should have small indentations and look rather like a pitted crater. At this point, cover the pan with a very tight-fitting lid and turn the heat as low as possible.

While the rice is boiling, prepare the rest of the dish. If you are using fresh peas, blanch them in boiling water for 2 minutes, then drain and set aside. With frozen peas, let them thaw at room temperature.

Heat a wok or large frying-pan and add the oil. Add the pork and stir-fry for 1 minute, then add the peas, the soy sauces, oyster sauce, salt and rice wine. Continue to cook for another 2 minutes, then add the spring onions. Put this cooked mixture on top of the rice and continue to cook over the lowest possible heat for another 15 minutes (the rice should cook for a total of 25 minutes). Serve at once; drizzle additional oyster sauce over the top of the casserole if you wish.

RICE WITH CHINESE SAUSAGE

*T*his southern Chinese peasant dish is one of my favourites. If you serve it with a vegetable, it makes a very satisfying, sustaining meal, and yet it is so quick and easy to prepare. While the rice and sausage are cooking, prepare a fast stir-fried vegetable dish and there you are! Try to get Chinese sausages for this recipe – they are so sweetly flavoured that they are well worth the search.

Left-overs from this dish can be swiftly converted into another tasty meal on the following day: simply stir-fry the rice and re-combine with the finely chopped sausages and some chopped spring onions and beaten eggs.

SHOPPING LIST
12 oz (350 g) Chinese sausages

PREPARATION TIME *5 minutes*

COOKING TIME *25 minutes*

SERVES 4–6

15 fl oz (400 ml) long-grain rice
1½ pints (900 ml) water
12 oz (350 g) Chinese sausages

Put the rice in a heavy pan with the water and bring it to the boil. Continue boiling for about 10 minutes or until most of the surface liquid has evaporated. While the rice is boiling, cut the sausages diagonally into 2 inch (5 cm) segments. By now the surface of the rice should have small indentations and look rather like a pitted crater. At this point place the sausages on the top of the rice, cover the pan with a very tight-fitting lid, turn the heat as low as possible and let the rice cook undisturbed for 15 minutes more. Serve immediately.

QUICK FRIED RICE

*I*f you prepare the rice beforehand, this dish takes but 16 minutes from wok to table. You can boil the rice hours or even days in advance and store it, well covered, in the refrigerator. This recipe is typical of the fried rice served in Chinese homes, with just a few simple seasonings to perk up the bland but congenial cereal. Serve it as part of a meal with a fast meat or poultry dish and your favourite salad. Alternatively, turn Quick Fried Rice into a speedy one-dish meal by adding left-overs.

SHOPPING LIST
  Fresh root ginger
  4 eggs

PREPARATION TIME *rice – 5 minutes;*
  Quick Fried Rice – 8 minutes

COOKING TIME *rice – 25 minutes;*
  Quick Fried Rice – 7–8 minutes

SERVES 4–6

15 fl oz (400 ml) long-grain rice
1½ pints (900 ml) water
2 tablespoons oil (preferably groundnut)
2 teaspoons salt
2 tablespoons coarsely chopped fresh root ginger
4 eggs, beaten

Put the rice in a heavy pan with the water and bring it to the boil. Continue boiling for about 10 minutes or until most of the surface liquid has evaporated. The surface of the rice should have small indentations and look rather like a pitted crater. At this point cover the pan with a very tight-fitting lid, turn the heat as low as possible and let the rice cook undisturbed for 15 minutes more. Remove from the heat and allow to cool thoroughly.

Heat a wok or large frying-pan, add the oil, salt and ginger and stir-fry for 1 minute. Now add the cooked rice and continue to stir-fry for another 5 minutes. Stir in the eggs and cook for 1 minute. Serve at once or allow to cool and serve at room temperature.

DESSERTS

*D*esserts are *not* the forte of Chinese cuisine; indeed, they are the one weak element in all of that venerable cookery. Why this is so is a complex question. That it is so is undeniable, so in this section I have kept to quick and easy Western themes but with a Chinese accent manifest in the emphasis on fruit. All the recipes are extremely easy to prepare and deliciously refreshing. The use of fruit is appropriate because of its ease of preparation, its versatility and its cleansing lightness after the more intense Chinese flavourings.

LITCHIS WITH PAPAYA SAUCE

*L*itchis are a sweet exotic fruit that is becoming more and more available in the West. Try to use fresh ones with this dramatic sauce for an elegant dessert fit for any occasion. The sauce can be prepared several hours in advance and refrigerated, tightly covered with cling film until you need it.

SHOPPING LIST
1 × 1 lb (450 g) papaya
1 lb (450 g) fresh or tinned
*   litchis*

PREPARATION TIME *15 minutes*

SERVES 4–6

1 × 1 lb (450 g) papaya
2 tablespoons sugar
1 lb (450 g) fresh or tinned
    litchis

Slice the papaya in half lengthways and remove the seeds. Peel away the skin and cut the flesh into slices. Purée the slices in a blender or food processor and stir in the sugar. If you are using fresh litchis, peel and stone them. If you are using tinned litchis, drain them well.

To serve, put some papaya sauce on each plate and then top with the litchis.

MANGO FOOL

*T*his rich but refreshing dessert brings a meal to a close with a Southeast Asian touch. Fresh ripe mangoes are irresistible.

SHOPPING LIST
1 lb (450 g) fresh mangoes
8 fl oz (250 ml) double or
*   whipping cream*

PREPARATION TIME *20 minutes*

SERVES 4

1 lb (450 g) fresh mangoes
2 tablespoons sugar
8 fl oz (250 ml) double or
    whipping cream

Peel and slice the mangoes, discarding the stones. Purée the fruit in a blender or food processor. Put the purée through a fine sieve and stir in the sugar. Whip the cream until it forms stiff peaks, then gently fold it into the mango purée. This dish will keep for 3–4 hours covered with cling film in the refrigerator.

STRAWBERRY OR RASPBERRY FOOL

When fresh strawberries and raspberries are in season, make the most of them. Try this delicious dessert: quick, easy and elegant.

SHOPPING LIST
*12 oz (350 g) fresh strawberries
or raspberries
8 fl oz (250 ml) double or
whipping cream*

PREPARATION TIME *8 minutes*

SERVES 4

12 oz (350 g) fresh strawberries
or raspberries
2 tablespoons sugar
8 fl oz (250 ml) double or
whipping cream

Purée the strawberries or raspberries in a blender or food processor. Stir in the sugar. Whip the cream until it forms stiff peaks, then gently fold it into the berry purée. This dish will keep for 3–4 hours covered with cling film in the refrigerator.

STRAWBERRIES WITH ORANGE LIQUEUR

This is a lovely coda to any meal, elegant and very easy to prepare. It can be made hours in advance. Serve it, perhaps with some plain biscuits or cream, as part of a meal for family or friends.

SHOPPING LIST
    8 oz (225 g) fresh strawberries

PREPARATION TIME *8 minutes plus 2
    hours' marinating*

SERVES 2

8 oz (225 g) fresh strawberries
3 tablespoons sugar
1 tablespoon orange liqueur

Clean and hull the strawberries. Toss them gently in a bowl with the sugar and orange liqueur. Cover with cling film and refrigerate for at least 2 hours before serving.

PAPAYA AND GRAPEFRUIT SALAD

*G*rapefruit are sometimes taken for granted, their tartness and sweetness overlooked in this age of more glamorous fare. But they take on new dimensions with this papaya companion and the result is a refreshing dessert dish. For more colour and elegance, add fresh strawberries or raspberries.

SHOPPING LIST
    1 × 1½ lb (700 g) papaya
    2 grapefruit
    1 lemon

PREPARATION TIME *15 minutes*

SERVES 4

1 × 1½ lb (700 g) papaya
2 grapefruit
2 tablespoons lemon juice
2 tablespoons sugar

Slice the papaya in half lengthways and remove the seeds. Peel away the skin and cut the flesh into slices. Peel the grapefruit and divide the flesh into segments. Arrange the fruits on a platter and sprinkle with the lemon juice and sugar. Cover tightly with cling film until you are ready to serve.

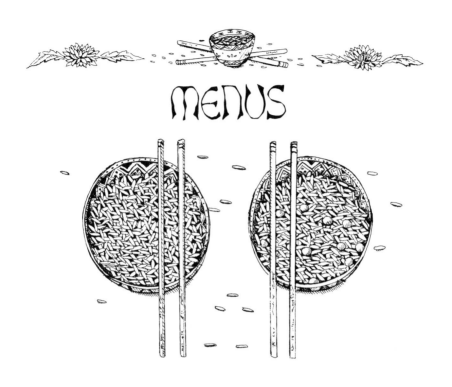

MENUS

COOKED AHEAD

Do-ahead Re-heatable Lamb Stew (pages 94–5)
or
Do-ahead Re-heatable Black Bean Spareribs (pages 90–1)
Elizabeth Chong's Noodle Salad (page 119)

SIMPLE FAMILY MEAL

Minced Turkey Patties (pages 63–4)
Bean Sauce Noodles (page 116)
Salad
Mango Fool (pages 126–7)

SUNDAY FAMILY DINNER

Chinese Barbecued Chicken (page 62)
Potatoes in Curry-Coconut Stew (page 111)
Salad
Fresh Fruit

TOO BUSY TO COOK

Fast Seafood Soup (pages 38–9)
Salad
Bread

DRINKS AND NIBBLES

Spicy Fried Cashew Nuts (page 29)
Crispy Prawns (page 30)

FAST LUNCHEON

Quick Orange-Lemon Chicken (pages 76–7)
Steamed Rice
Salad
Fresh Fruit

ONE-DISH MENUS FOR A CROWD

Hot and Spicy Rice with Beef (page 121)
or
Spicy Rice Noodles with Mussels (page 117)
or
Fast Curried Fish Stew (pages 45–6)
Steamed Rice

Pre-theatre Dinner

5-minute Fish Cooked on a Plate (page 53)
Bright Pepper and Green Bean Stir-fry (page 113)
Salad
Fresh Fruit

Midweek Blues Menu

Tri-colour Soup (page 39)
Stir-fried Pork with Litchis (page 86)
Steamed Rice

Rainy-day Dinner

Curried Baked Chicken Thighs (pages 73–4)
Steamed Rice
Fresh Fruit

Light Supper for after Theatre

Grilled Prawns with Fresh Coriander and Ginger Sauce (pages 24–5)
Cold Cucumber Salad (page 28)
Quick Chinese Chicken Salad (pages 60–1)
Strawberry Fool (page 127)

Romantic Dinner

Chicken and Watercress Soup (pages 36–7)
Steamed Salmon with Black Bean Sauce (pages 48–9)
Potatoes with a Fresh Coriander, Spring Onion and Sesame Oil Dressing
(page 107)
Strawberries with Orange Liqueur (pages 127–8)

ELEGANT MENU FOR AN UNEXPECTED GUEST

Fast Curried Fish Stew (pages 45–6)
or
15-minute Steak (page 92)
Green Rice (page 120)
Salad
Mango Fool (pages 126–7)

MENU-ON-THE-RUN

Minced Pork, Pea and Rice Casserole (pages 122–3)

QUICK AND EASY ENTERTAINING

Tomato Ginger Soup (pages 37–8)
10-minute Salmon with Spring Onion Sauce (pages 46–7)
Oyster Sauce Asparagus (page 102)
Fresh Fruit and Cheese

SUNDAY NIGHT SUPPER

Fast Spicy Meat Sauce and Rice Noodles (page 80)
Tossed Green Salad
Papaya and Grapefruit Salad (page 128)

MENU OUT OF THE LARDER

Crispy Chicken in Garlic-Ginger Sauce (pages 65–6)
Stir-fried Peas with Fresh Coriander and Spring Onions (page 106)
Steamed Rice

INDEX

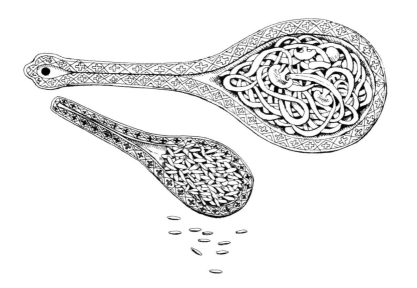